ORGANIC INK

VOLUME ONE

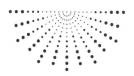

EDITED BY J.E. FELDMAN

Editing & Formatting by Dragon Soul Press
Cover Art by Covers By Juan

POETS

ZOEY XOLTON

BIOGRAPHY

Zoey Xolton is a published Australian writer of Dark Fantasy, Paranormal Romance and Horror. She is also a proud mother of two, and is married to her soul mate. Outside of her family, writing is her greatest passion. She is especially fond of short fiction and is working on releasing her own collections in future. To find out more, please visit her website!

THE DEVIL'S MISTRESS

With hands youthful beyond her years,
Into the cauldron she offers her fears.
A child unborn, not living, yet dead.
Three words longed for, but never said.
She stirs her cauldron, clock-wise first,
This precious brew to slake her thirst
For knowledge, for life, for beauty and time.
When will the dark bells of Hell chime?
Calling her home, to her king,
To the Halls of Eternal Darkness where she might sing.
Of murders and madness, spells and curses,
Songs of wickedness to mar holy verses.
She whispers her vow, her solemn pledge,
And from the cauldron she does dredge,
A mortal skull, filled to the brim
With broken dreams and sins most grim.
Down her throat the turgid potion goes,
How many more dark moons has she left?
Only the devil knows.

A MATE FOR THE DARK SOUL

In the darkness, resides my soul,
Black, hard and burning, like fragments of coal.
Twisted and tortured, it yearns for a mate,
For an end to loneliness it desires to sate.
Where once there was joy, there is malice and pain,
Like a desert in spring, it pines for the rain.
To feel naught but constant heartache and dread,
Has left my spirit wounded and dead.
Harken, find me, I long for your touch,
The misery, the agony, has become too much.
Save me, claim me, wrap me in love,
No more devils, but angels from above.
Were I to change, to alter myself and be,
Something changed, different and free,
Could you see the truth that lies within?
Past years of heresy and grave mortal sin?
If I held you close, under my black wing,
Peace I would find, and my soul could sing.

AN ODE TO BLOOD

Blood is the rose,
Blood is the stone.
Blood is the garden,
Blood is the throne.
Blood is the day,
Blood is the night.
Blood is the hunger,
Blood is the fright.
Blood is the word,
Blood is the song.
Blood is the right,
Blood is the wrong.
Blood is the why,
Blood is the reason.
Blood is the truth,
Blood is the treason.
Blood is the start,
Blood is the end.
Blood is the sinner,
Blood is the friend.

THE GUILT OF CONSCIENCE

Silence emanated all around,
Her bare feet cold upon the ground.
To go left, or to go right?
Into everlasting peace, or darkest night?
Where was her bed and crackling fire?
Where was her king, her beloved sire?
"How came I to be here?" aloud she said.
"To my crossroads you have come,
Because you are dead."
"And who are you, to speak to me?" asked the queen.
"I am Hekate, the goddess of the in-between."
"What should I do?"
"That is up to you.
It is not I who judge, that is your burden to bear."
"Throughout my life, I have not been fair.
Murder and mayhem, I have wrought.
Surely my soul, the Devil has bought."
"There is no devil, but the one in the heart,
You are your own devil, your own work of art."
"So if I wish peace, I can have it you say,
Despite the fact, that I forsook the day?

To embrace the night and all her dark,
Never again, to hear the lark..."
"All manner of creatures I have seen,
Gods, shifters, vampires, fae and everything in-between.
All come to my crossroads at the end of their time,
Looking for reason, hope or rhyme.
But the path you walk, is up to you,
Do you be false, or do you be true?
In the end, it's all the same to me,
Hades claims all life,
For his beloved queen, Persephone."

HAIKUS

A single red rose,
    A memory in time lost,
    A lover's last kiss.

Forgotten is she
    Now that her last breath is drawn,
    Her grave untended.

The moon at night glows,
    The wolf a shadow.
    Blood stains the white snow.

Fallen the old tree,
    It sings songs of memory.
    Rings tell dark stories.

In my broken heart

My love yearns for release.
With a knife it ends.

The blackbird it sings,
  Of death and bitter things.
  I await the dawn.

Gone is the bright hope,
  Replaced by blackest fear.
  Give us a reason.

Summer sun is gone,
  Autumn leaves are falling down,
  Winter will soon come.

MELINDA KUCSERA

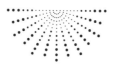

BIOGRAPHY

Melinda Kucsera writes fantastic short stories, novels, and books when dragons and armies of fictional characters aren't kidnapping her. (They do, on occasion, rescue her.) She's also written short stories and novellas in iambic pentameter with sonnets instead of paragraphs. Every scribe has quirks. For more books by Melinda Kucsera, visit her website. Visit Welcome Characters for more dramatic rescues and magical mayhem. Every week's a new adventure.

A NOVEL IN VERSE

Everywhere he looked spring had sprung green, gold
with clear running streams no longer ice-choked.
Nights still froze his balls off but leave the wold
he would to see Shayari 'fore he croaked.
Nothing tied him here since his wife had gone.
His kids now grown no longer wanted him
around, an inconvenience he'd become.
He set off that morn adjusting his brim,
to hide the tear tracing his grizzled cheek.
He put his home of five decades behind
and headed for the last time to that creek
which marked the end of home. No time to whine
about loss, giving that his back, he turned
and in his breast, curiosity burned.
Henneth passed the creek, started up the vale's
wall seeking its rim, and not one son run
up to ask him where he's bound or to rail
at him for leaving home to have some fun.
Bare branches scratch the aquamarine sky
as he pauses on the valley rim, breath
caught by a village planted in the sky.

The treehouses, suspended on a breath,
nestled in enchanted oaks, connected
by ladders and bridges—a delicate
tangle teaming with life, disconnected
now, his home no more, that village he quits.
He's departing on his last adventure.
It's his first and only solo venture.
Henneth hadn't gone far 'fore he heard voices
that weren't real friendly, so he hid behind
those boles. Creep and skulk he did, 'till choices
guaranteed no fighting of any kind.
When Henneth stepped out he saw a tinker
with his cart and an old brass watch in hand.
"I've lost my ride," said Tinker man, hoofprints
attested to his word, "Damn spooky land."
This man, half his age, wanted Hen to sprint
after a high-spirited bunch of beasts?
No damned way! Hen opened his mouth to say,
but the look the tinker gave sent him east
trotting after the damned mule anyway.
Hen found the beast tangled in a thicket.
For his labor, he earned a gold ticket.
The tinker's cart clattered off as Hen looked
at the gold ticket in his hand wond'ring
what to do with it. He felt a bit rooked
by the whole deal. His peachy skin stings
from where thorns scratched and his compensation?
No balm to soothe his skin just a solid
gold plate inscribed with gibberish. No ration,
no sign of legal tender for stolid
Henneth making his way through th'enchanted
forest–at least they've left off their mischief,
those trees, long enough to take for granted
that their quietude will last. Though mischief's
never far from their boles, and even now
their restless grows from root to bent bough…

Angels danced in cold atomic-orange
dust from days long past, whirling through sunbeams
cleaving the darkening sky like lace bridges
leading away from loss. Hen paused; streams
of glory wend past, ensnare his sight, fix
his eyes on another sunset e'er beloved
Shayari, whose gasps rise as night fixes
what day broke, dials up cold for beloved
winter whose bite, though remembered, hasn't left
just yet even though spring is on the move.
Henneth sat there on a ridge, in a cleft,
protected from winds' frigid bite, this rock groove
itself none-too-warm but enough for night's
repose and down below, a road's in sight.
Hen drank tepid tea heated by crystal-
fire though truth be told, he should have bought
a larger warming stone 'cause red lumir's
got properties that constrain its much-sought
heat, which this chill season does require.
Calendar be damned; it says spring has sprung
but out there in the wild, winter's still mired.
Cursive clouds, sky's writing, tells of storms flung
down from Storm King's northern tower, that sad
creature whose punitive power swallows
aquamarine dawn now stormy gray-clad,
an affirmation of snow tomorrow.
Henneth gathers his things, prepares to flee
the storm's coming for a nice cave to be.
Henneth scrambled down from his rocky perch
as eagles took wing to sky-dance with storm clouds.
He hoped their antics didn't cause the clouds to burst.
Sharp of talon those birds were and so proud.
The Storm King, legend claims, had a fondness
for such majestic birds who dwelt year-round
in Shayari's enchanted boughs, honest.
Henneth slid down the crag's steep side but found

no road or path, and no sign that these miles
had e'er been trod, just walls of trees, no homes
hung in the their boughs and no village for miles.
He had hallucinated the path home
for none now wended through that tangled, wild
wood surrounding him. Shelter, he must find.
Into the deep forest he traipsed, his heart
beat an arrhythmic tattoo that he marched
to as ancient trees closed in around this part.
They spanned a thousand-feet from where ants marched
to brush the sky and paint all in shadow
here below. Though here and there, they glowed bright
those sun-dappled branches, in mourning, bowed
and bent in a dance that show'red all in light,
and all this happened at the wind's behest
and by its gentle caress which tricked eyes
and minds alike, taking both from the test
half-hid by wakening grass, which though high,
can't contain the item there stashed which reaches
for Henneth as he, for shelter searches.
At last, just as snow sifted from the sky
Henneth spotted a dark hole in the ground.
He hurried towards it and tripped with a cry.
Something hard caught his foot. What had he found?
Feeling along the cold ground, his fingers
touched ice and recoiled as a glow bathed all,
not in any natural hue triggered
by magick'd trees, but pure white light, whose call
echoed in bone, beat with his heart and wrapped
his fingers around a warming sword's grip.
An enchanted blade, its crystal-point trapped
his gaze. Words coruscated; meaning dripped
slow as honey into his mind and know
he what he beheld—a Guardian Blade, wow.
But how could he, man of fifty plus springs
be chosen to wield a blade of ancient

power? About whose bearers bards oft sing?
Yet here in hand was one such blade, ancient,
virile, in the hand of a nobody
from nowhere special, decades
past his prime, who had ventured out to see
what he could of the world before his shade
ripped free and joined his dead wife but not soon.
While he'd sat dumbstruck, the Storm King's fury
had built to quite a bad blow, like a loon
he sat admiring a sword that can't be
his; someone important must have dropped it.
To its guardian, he must return it.
First to find shelter lest he be laid low
by that bad blow poised to drop feet of snow.
Up Henneth got and now hurried away
searching for a dry place with walls to stay.
It stank of asparagus, but the cave's
pulchritude drew him on; its stone sparkled
like diamond dust scattered 'cross the concave
walls. 'Neath the forest's feet, they bore up marbled
by granite and darkened lumir revealed
by sword's light, and the sight made Hen forget
the stench 'till a baby's cry made him reel.
Echoes of that cry caught his breath as threats
of never finding the child mounted.
Tunnels twisted, crisscrossed, at cliffs ended,
but he kept searching though it amounted
to nothing as the storm broke. The wind wended
past, freezing him as he looked in each cave.
He must find that babe or he'd rant and rave.
The more Henneth searched, the more the cave-walls
wavered, transforming as he inhaled perfume
where floated rose's kiss and a promised fall
onto a bow-decked bed, veiled by no doom,
just a mosquito net; no love mirrored
there, just a door closing and a demon,

pink carnations in hand, standing silvered
by a garden path. Henneth's reason's
flown as he follows. His sword's grown heavy
in his hand; his thoughts stall out and their thrum
quiets. His ability to resist
the enchanter wanes; the sword's growing hum
can't break the spell Hen's under. It enlists
aid by reaching out to she who slumbers,
Anonymous, she trips the lock's tumblers...

For most of history, Anonymous
was a woman. She rises from the ground
in disregard; in pastel she's all trussed
up and corseted. In courage, she's found.
No weapons for her, she's got a bowl full
of buttons and thread enough to button
up the foulest enchanter; the rightful
cave's owner, it's her energy that's spun
into this farce; in theory, one good shove
ought to catapult the fool-captive free.
She's the element of surprise, this dove,
not that she needs it. She was young and free
when history was a caterwauling
baby—or is that a real babe crying?

She pauses to listen. Those echoes fall
silent; they risk not her ire, and the urge
to check dies out as she walks to stop all
the madness that's about to here converge.
A minute's run puts her deep into spells
any man would have to hack through with swords.
A basket of pale purple pears compels
her to pick it up and toss it toward
the emaciated thing practicing
dark arts, making it scream as its matter
disintegrates on contact thus cleansing

the air, leaving his victim in tatters.
"What just happened?" Hen asked though shaking still.
"Buddy, you followed a thing made of swill."

Henneth tried to process her words but no
sense could he make of them not from his view.
She yawned and stretched, "if you want food, you know
how to cook it. Grate's over there. I'm through
here. Stay as long as your gear hold out, Dear."
She left then and stepped into the Storm King's
snowy tantrum. At which she paused to sneer,
"This the best you got, you cotton-crowned King,
you moldy, cobweb-addled, beardless twit!"
The wind snatched her words and flung them at its King
whose apoplectic fury loosed a blitz—
frosty hounds bent on a long glacial freeze.
She seized them, hitched them to a cart and roared,
"I'm woman, hear me roar." As off she soared.

Henneth watched all this in perplexity.
Though bards had long maintained Millennium's
Children, known for their anonymity,
oft dispensed with names. 'Future's premium,'
they said, but that seemed sad to Hen, that name
should be forgot as pow'r massed to protect
one's independence forgoing all fame,
but then what did he know 'bout detection?
Perhaps the path she trod was link enough
to the world that names were just letters-read,
their meaning carried forth while off the bluff,
the letter was tossed never to be read
'gain by anyone, not e'en the owner,
who has no interest in a loaner.

The sword's glow pulled Hen, like beaver to den,
his mind to back to the reason for this quest.

Listen he did but no baby's cry then
did he hear that hour or the next. That pressed
him to search as the air chilled, but he found
no baby, not 'round that last bend, just a kid
goat, curled up and freezing. It'd made the sound.
He had no milk to give, but warm the kid
he did as he munched dried venison, tough
as leather and teeth-crackingly salty,
but food nonetheless. He drank from rough
streams that formed their own lanes while his faulty
mind worked through it all until blanket-wrapped,
Henneth and the goat kid, dreamed while they napped.
Twilight's darkening veil surprised Henneth
with a wind soughing through spare, still-bare boughs
dressed in white, delicate wet tufts. His breath
misted as he tried to figure out how
he'd misplaced a day. The goat kid poked its
head out of Hen's shirt, bleated denials.
Its fleece body stayed nestled. The visit
had taken too long, and he'd walked far, riled
by the whole enchanter incident, veiled
'neath boughs not realizing that day had spun
itself out. Now, he stood by a field jailed
by razor wire and the nearly-set sun.
Winter's last gasp, frosted goodbyes tendered
in its retreat, such beauty here rendered.
No cover though, just a blanket of snow,
roofed o'er by a purpling ripple replete
with stars. Their apology? A light show
where wishes streak across the sky and greet
wishers as they fall free. Those bright cinders
from Heaven's nexus come to share and bowl
o'er watchers from this low level. Tinder
for future's fire, those anonymous souls,
stargazers who share their wishes with stars
who dash and flee in nick-of-the-time peace.

Cheeks flushed from wind's caress, Hen watches stars
dance o'er that fenced-off field, and time ceases
to exist. Those bright stars lure him to climb
o'er barbed wire to stare at the sky's long limb.
The goat kid kicked as Hen, without breaking stride,
cut across that snowy field; 'tween starlight
and sword's glow, the goat kid's form shuddered, tried
to triumph o'er spells layered out of sight.
When light subsided, Henneth held that lost
babe he'd heard crying in the cave; the one
he'd left to cold death when it had stayed lost.
Not a bust then his quest, but what's he done?
He's no milk for a babe, and no trick will
evict hunger from an empty tummy.
Hen swore at the enchanter whose skill
hid the babe underground like mummies
of old while still alive. What a mess, and
what's he to do without a helping hand?
A night camp 'neath stars was out of question.
Not with a babe who'd suffered God knew what.
He'd have to find a vale, a way station
or some itinerant woman's camp but
where to find a wet nurse who's handy? No
more music of the spheres tonight nor dances
with the stars, not when he scented more snow.
Henneth's left wrist ached with its swift advance.
Lights broke yonder dark ahead, heartening
Hen. He added to his earlier list,
munching buttery bread. At his heels barking,
loneliness ran as night closed its cold fist.
Hen crashed through snow drifts on that frozen field
with only uncertainty as a shield.
Henneth crossed the field that razor-wire fenced,
those barbs its only defense, 'neath a sky
pricked by star glow that fell and here condensed.
He saw 'lil folk weave starlight as they fly.

Underfoot, frost makes spiny acanthus-
leaved iced flowers of all as it settles.
His mind scrolls through the Litany to suss
out the Little Folks' name as frost petals
crunch underfoot. Allies, Enemies and
Other Folk were named in that Litany.
Which are these folk, Allies or Enemies?
"What do you think?" he asks the babe, tiny
in his arms, who just stares, "not enemies,
they're too fair, and enemies are foul, so
allies. But if I'm wrong, we'll pay with woe!"
Hen found them in the section for Allies.
Anandarwen, the Little Folk, lucky
to those who see them; they're quite a surprise.
In the deep woods, they thrive where magic's key.
Henneth approached them with caution, mindful
of his advantage over a lissome
sprite one-sixth his height, known to be bashful.
A scream made all th'Anandarwen flee from
the bulging fence. Barbs stabbed the falling dark
that cloaks stars' distant light. Too black to see,
the Dreaming Hour drops its shroud. All is stark.
Night takes on depth, tangles Hen's feet. His knees
bend. He struggles to get free. Claws scratch, tear,
knock him down, and he hits his head and fears.
Th'Anandarwen cower in their bowers.
Made of woven grass, their nests, jays envy.
The Undeem skip them since their loathsome pow'r
won't penetrate the leaf-mold and ivy
with frozen drops of spiderweb-caught dew.
The babe cried as time elapsed and threatened
to completely unspool, as the haunts drew
more foul creatures to the field, not their den.
The Hollowed Oak lay safely hid in star
glow, moonlight and all that's fairest at night.
Time unaccountable passed 'fore a star

flared white amid the tufted snow. It's sight
made the Undeem cry and skitter away
to wait for th'end of tumultuous day.
When sun's light crested the Enchanted trees
that edged their field, the Anadarwen rose
from hiding. A man sprawled in their grass sea.
Trapped beneath him, a Guardian sword throws
the light that drew them from their safe 'lil nests.
Dawn, that pearl, hasn't rolled down the East Reaches.
Mighty Night held dominion and that sets
butterfly wings aflutter and teaches
them not to trust light alone to shield them.
They gathered around the man, Anasril
touched his hand, shook her head, "he's no golem."
"Not yet anyway," challenged old Basril,
"You know what becomes of those the Undeem
touch, and he was so touched by them it seems."
Anasril faced them, "he's a Guardian.
We must aid him!" she said, receiving nods.
Shouts of, 'for Vanatium', Guardian
most revered by her people, sent from God
to save them from the Alou'ear, a mad
beast that had taken to hunting their kind.
His remembered deeds earned for this plain-clad
man, a piping song that called all her kind
from the Hollowed Tree to come and carry.
Lights blazed on the wind, spheres cast by wing-glow,
as the Anadarwen army ferried
the felled Guardian from this scene of woe.
Anasril glanced back at the broken fence's
wire-webs. Captured starlight was no defense.
They flew, struggled to keep the Guardian
from dragging. Their wings beat humming-bird fast,
but still he's sagging; his cloak's draggin'.
His weight pulls his small bearers 'till at last,
gravity wins, and Hen lands in the snow.

Exhausted, his foot-tall rescuers pant
and gasp as they rest their tired wings, and woe
to the giant pain-in-their-wings who can't
get up and follow them to some shelter.
Anasril bit her lip; they hadn't carried
him far, He was too heavy, but shelter
he needed. Her breath was misting, carried
on the wind's sigh southwards towards the Groundling's
abode where silver water falls, singing...
Anasril shook out her wings, blue as night's
retreating back, as distant dawn rises
o'er the East Reaches for real, out of sight
for now, though soon to reveal its gold prize.
She gave the crumpled Guardian a glance
that steeled her spine and took with her his sword's
glow, locked safe in mem'ry's box as she danced
with the wind, making its current her own.
A shining pebble, it catapulted
her, leaving wings' glow to see, since moon's frown
lends little light to the predawn tumult.
E'en with snow reflecting her fairy-light,
blue shadows, drawn to obscure, cover sites.
Furious wing-beats follow the swift shade
that o'ertook her. He stopped and hovering
in front of her, blocked her flightpath; dismayed,
she regarded Chero. His silver wings
were velvety as a moth's, and they beat
an angry tattoo matched by mad slanted
eyes whose epicanthic fold seemed a treat
for her fingers to trace, but he's ranting.
She held her hands to keep them from touching
Gathevral's heir, and she listened instead.
"—they're still out here," Chero said, reminding
her about the Undeem whom she dreaded.
"Wait until first light for this mad errand
when light blinds them, do whatever you planned."

"I can't wait that long. He might die without
help, and we're too small to do anything."
She needed a mendicant but doubted
she'd find one wandering around with things
like th'Undeem about, and far away
lived the Mountain Folk whose herb craft might save.
"They're the closest help I can get," she swayed.
Weaving starlight into defenses gave
her no rest, and the night's toil caught up fast.
Chero's eyes narrowed but 'fore he renewed
the debate, she swerved 'round him and flew fast
as hummingbirds zip from flower to rue.
Now she's racing the clouds from field to glen.
Where water falls, hope and help make their den.
Anasril drifted like a dandelion
seed on the wind; her crinoline petti-
coats belled 'round her like a rose's scion.
Chero paced her, and dawn tossed confetti
clouds for the rising sun to coruscate.
Ahead two mountains kissed and water fell
in a pale rivulets that formed delicate
veils whose hems ruffled the riffle where dwelled,
somewhere nearby, an enclave of Groundlings.
The 'where' part vexed Anasril's tired mind
as she landed face-first on the frost-kissed
earth and ended up in a dirty bind.
Chero's landing, while not a graceless spill,
left him sweaty and staring at the rill.
He squat beside her as she lay panting,
listening to the falling water sing
a lullaby to the setting moon, King
of fallen pantheons, 'till the cold sting
of the chill morning forced her to move on.
Chero's more practical garb had survived
their hurried flight better than hers; she yawned.
"They're in there," Chero said, "I hear their hive."

He pointed, but the water-veil refused
to part as she shuddered at thought of wet
wings and the ice-cold drenching to ensue.
She started when Chero lifted her, set
course and without delay, they were flying
toward falls that seemed to beat a warning.
Chero looped around the falls and behind,
darting into the mouth of a cave lit
by wing-glow alone leaving darkness twined
with apprehension. Dark blinded and bit
into her courage as they alighted.
A skeleton's eyeless sockets mocked where
it reclined by the slick entrance; its sight
unnerved Anasril who'd hoped for aid here.
Chero hopped onto its head; his boots clicked
on the bleached skull as he examined marks
scratched on the bone; he touched a tripwire, flicked
it too, extinguishing her hopes with snark.
The hidden trap didn't trigger at his touch.
"To know how this was done, I would give much."
"It's not—" she broke off, swallowed, "of the dark?"
Chero shook his head. "No it's protective.
It's meant to drive off those here on a lark."
He gave her a crooked smile; effective
that, it shorted out her fear, and she smiled.
"How do you know that weaving of bone and wire
is safe—it's very odd," she shuddered, riled
at this thing, and possibly also tired.
Chero didn't answer as a shadow slid
over his face; his whole clan had flown miles
uncounted, migrating far in a bid
for safety here in Shayari's green miles
where enchanted forests covered all save
the hundred mountains, whose views people craved.
"We should go. They don't know we're here," he said
jumping down to the ground to save his wings.

Anasril flew on and landed ahead;
this time, with some grace thanks to rested wings.
They walked down the tunnel's stone throat, tiny
in comparison, in step as it grew
steeper; her mind on the wounded man; He
must stay alive; his life was a gift through
which life kept its promise of fair play, and
change, bringer of tears, must bow and present
the choice to flee as the enchanted lands
of the west fall to mortals who resent
magic in all its forms. They would repeal
it here if Guardians didn't keep it sealed.
Light spilled in a gold wash; its rays arrowed
around the next bend bounced by reflective
shields mounted high on the tunnel's narrowed,
jagged walls; such an ameliorative
sight that light cutting through the cave's false dark.
Outside the sun's face shined; Anasril feels
its sacrosanct warmth on her soul and hope sparks.
Maybe her quest is not in vain; she steals
a glance at Chero; he's peering around
the next bend, squinting into refracted
light. Then with an irreverent shrug, he bounds
into light, which she too is attracted.
Light blinded her 'till her eyes adjusted
and what wonders she saw, she mistrusted.
Nothing hindered them, but they stared a while.
Cut into the huge cavern's roof, skylights
poured the spring sun into a crystal phial
suspended by a silver basket right
over the middle of the cavern where
dwelt a cluster of cottages all carved
from pink feldspar around a central square.
The phial pulsed, showering white light on carved
homes, ramps and a small lake where swans glided.
Above that blue-green water, blue-violet and

white stone inlaid in a mosaic spread
o'er the domed roof 'round whose oculus spanned
a very close approximation of
night's shades gathering like flocks of dark doves.
Too busy staring, they didn't see the swans
trade their underground lake for a stone ramp
curving up to where they stood gaping. Wan
and drawn from hours of toil, both swamped
by the incredible place, they didn't know
what to do next. The swans' expectant eyes
and the soft backs they presented goaded
them into action. Chero caught her eye,
shrugged, then offered her a hand, which she took
wishing that hand had offered marriage bands
instead. She sat on feathers; an arm hooked
around her waist, Chero's; she squeezed his hand.
His father wouldn't approve; she pushed that thought
out, concentrated on the aid she sought.
The swans' smooth gait had Anasril nodding
off as the pair, one black and one white, slid
into blue-green water around which springs
flowers and herbs and down below fish hid
as the swans' shadow left ripples behind.
After they'd swam to the opposite shore,
the swans left the lake, padded off to find
their mistress, Eloaysa at the core
of this little town, its most respected
citizen and the best person to handle
magical visitors unexpected.
They genuflected; she set the candle
down and closed the loculus, crossed her heart
then turned from the stone altar with a start.
"What have you brought?" Eloaysa bent, looked
at the two humanoid creatures blinking
from their interrupted rest; children looked
at her, neither more'n a foot tall, clinging

to each other with innocent eyes; wings,
butterfly-like, whose glow gave their kind a-
way: Anandarwen. But what thing could bring
the pair to Bayasheru? Far away
for lil' ones to go; they ne'er left their glen.
The female with bluish wings told her tale.
Her handsome companion stayed quiet when
she asked questions, but the end of the tale
left Eloaysa shaking her head. Nothing
her folk could do; they're too small for this thing.
"You need the Tall Folk—mountain men—" she waved
southwards towards Mount Rayastill and then eastwards
to the tree-top town of Aries and saved
for last the vale-cities quite far westwards.
A rare Groundling stood three-and-a-half-feet tall
but not her, she stood three-feet exactly.
The girl roused at this opposition; all
fire now that her quest was in danger, she
said the one word that changed everything.
"He's a Guardian! You must help him, now!"
Yes, she must help him who protected kings
and every good Shayarin too but how?
She straightened, went to the bell, and its chime
warned her neighbors it was meeting time.
Anasril watched the Groundlings gather 'round
the bell-ringer; her graying ringlets spilled from
a blue-violet kerchief as ceased all sounds
bringing the meeting to order. No crumb
for the messengers whose windowsill-perch
let them view the curly heads gathered there
to discuss their quest's fate, and if their search
for aid was in vain. Anasril sat there
arms around her knees, while Chero waited.
A many-legged shadow dragged things behind
as it scaled the blue-violet plaited
curtain, whose intricate folds she'd ne'er find

again; 'twas a lost art form but she'd no
mind to pay to curiosity though.
The shadow morphed into a spider leg
that hooked the sill, then another and swung
its hairy bod up next to Chero's leg.
The spider rubbed 'gainst Chero; behind hung
a web-wrapped parcel he detached with care.
The arachnid pancaked; its legs quivered
with bliss as he petted his pet spider.
Eight eyes regarded her; she didn't shiver.
For their silk webs, her people raised spiders.
Those spiders weren't hairy or smart like
Chero's pet, in whose eyes intelligence
gleamed; she tore open the bundle and psyched,
lifted out a feast, and all thought of whence
Chero came to Shayari and why flew
out of her mind at her first taste of blue.
Nectar rolled down her throat in a sweet, slow
cascade that dripped to her empty belly
filling it up and her beau; they won't know
for a while yet whether help was likely.
Exhaustion claimed them, and they curled up 'neath
blankets from Chero's pack. Chibi stood watch,
her eight eyes en garde; her spinnerets sheathed.
Anasril woke to a bumping cart splotched
with things; though swept clean, on it, her hopes rest
that it'd carry a Guardian; she grinned.
Chero sat on the driver's box's backrest;
Eight eyes protruded from his pack, legs twined
'round his neck–hairy spider legs—they tipped
her off to how Chibi'd come on this trip.
She floated over and joined him but sight
of a dozen Groundlings, eight men and four
women, that marched beside gave her a fright.
Beneath their tough soles, ice crackled like fore-
arm bones as they hot-footed it across

a frozen stream; an army followed now.
Dare she trust them? Her heart clenched with hope's loss.
Yes, her quest was true, but Chero's creased brow
gave her pause 'till his dark eyes captured hers.
In their depths, she found trust; her chest eased;
she breathed and sat beside him. The wheels whirred,
spokes blurred as the wagon rolled; it didn't seize.
She leaned into Chero and let him guide
them through the forest on hope's rick'ty ride.
They walked by lumir light, those bright crystals
held in the hand, affixed to wands, seated
in gilt wire cages that suspend crystal
glow from necklace, ring, anklet or beaded
into clothes or hairpins. They are walking
haloed in white light that's pure to protect
from falling shadows and evening's rising.
Its black tide brings bitter cold that rejects
spring's coming or life's affirming breath puffed
out in clouds that hang in sunset's first blush.
A hush falls with the brick red sun; rebuffed
by lengthening day and lingering flush
of crepuscular light, the Undeem wait
to stalk the night 'neath th'enchanted forest's
boughs, where giant trees dream in season's rest.
She cradled the taken babe in shadowed
arms; she of th'Undeem, this babe mortal-
born of a human woman, out in snow—
unforgivable—and her act of small
courage to swipe that child from uncaring
hands? Equally unforgivable. So
hide the child she must from the uncaring
of her people. First, clean and feed, then oh,
what should she do? Find a place, warm, hidden
but where? Where can she hide this little gift?
He's snuggling into a hole grief-ridden
in her heart. A hole punched by death's dark rift

that chasm even the undead Undeem
can't cross where her child waits to be redeemed.
Her heart still cries for her lost child, dead these
many years, 'till her arms held this babe near.
On the table. a tarot deck lies, teases
her with its promise of futures made clear.
She flips the top card o'er; the High Priestess
regards her with serenity in her eyes.
She sits at the crossroads of consciousness,
the moon's daughter, the high priestess, who spies
hidden truths and serves as imag'nation's
guardian, intuition's friend and all
that the Undeem lack in their perception.
She cradles the babe; her shoulders drop; all
hope of keeping him collapse as time brings
more chances for discovery's shrill ring.
His contented smile enchant'd her as no
other ever has. For him she defies
custom to the core, swaddles the baby so
no one will know, wrapping him in the guise
of her people—spun shadow riven from
night's falling veil where starless truth belies
day's blushing descent, and moon's crescent comes
to add its smile to the blue, dusky sky.
Snug, warm and fed, the babe, a crescent forms,
pressing close to her beating heart that tries
to rip her from the Undeems' shapeless dark to form
a woman with no flesh, just shadowed lies;
she was known long ago as Undreal.
Her essence he pulls, making her 'gain real.
Discordant screams send her flying as dread
stalks the ever-night lands of the Undeem's
abode—a shadow plane where night rests. Wed
to its n'er-changing cycle, night's bed seems
to lie far from mortal eyes 'till its rise,
when sun's brick-red setting reveals the cracks

that man hammered in balance's despised
hold on nature's and magic's leashes. Hack
at it with sword and axe in the west; fell
enchanted trees and break magic's dominion
so men might rise, but they forget that spells
don't fall to metal or poor opinion.
What magic made, only magic can break.
The fools made doors through which the Undeem sneak.
To such a crack, she rushes into brown
lands where only stumps remain and give no
protection from orange skies' burning throne.
Pillars of smoke mark war's progress; it sows
the seeds of future destruction, but care
she can't as sun's lingering light sparks fire
on her shadow raiment; flee to what's fair
she must; so dive into night's amplifier,
she does, moving deeper into blue dusk.
Jumping from shadow to shadow, and mile
to mile, she makes swift progress east through husks
of what was until Shayari's green miles,
protected by Guardians, magic's refuge,
she reaches ahead of Undeem's deluge.
Through enchanted boles, she sees a party
whose lumir-lit halo glimmers and hurts
her eyes, making her turn aside, and she
becomes the target for the Undeem's hunt
that night leaving the party of Groundlings
and their Anandarwen guides to proceed
in peace to prosecute their quest's ending.
While for Undreal, riven from the blasphemed
Undeem's unseen hordes, her quest has begun.
A quest that rests on the sweet-sleeping brow
of the babe clasped in her arms as she runs.
Shadows steal 'cross her path, but she's not cowed.
She's got a babe to protect and now raise.
For that, she who was lately damned, gives praise.

Anasril stirred when Chero took sudd'n flight.
He shot across the field to a great tree.
Blest long ago, the tree collects starlight.
It shimmers silver, rises to a V.
Its great limbs reach for the sky, touch the stars
whose small light powers its protective charms.
There flies an army sent from father to bar
access to this field, and they have come armed.
Snow-drops poked hopeful green heads through frosted
stems around their tree in that grassy sea.
They presaged spring, which winter'd accosted.
Old Storm King had bit deep for this to be.
The cold burned his wings; he missed milder climes.
He could only visit them in dream-time.
For gone they were now as the earth's magic
recedes back to its home in Shayari's
seeds, her sleeping buds, spring's coming magic.
Deforestation in the west left three
options for Chero's people: stay and die,
fly east to where forests and magic thrives
or survive deprived of magic and vie
for dwindling resources where war still thrives.
Chero's father chose flight and migration
back to where their ancestors first breathed life
to their line and left behind damnation.
He still heard the clang/clash of fighting rife
with screams, smelt death's fecal stench, tasted
ash choking th'air o'er land that'd been once chaste.
He pushed such thoughts aside, breathed Shayari's
pure air, spiked with pine and scented with snow.
The West was gone; East was his home, and he
had a squad of fear-crazed fairies to throw
off the chase, convince them that those coming
after him were allies for the moment.
As he'd hoped when he had sensed them, seeing
him confused them and they paused for comment.

Their instructions hadn't included a run-
in with the very person they'd been sent
to find, and that gave Chero time to run
through the adventure he'd had while absent.
His father's lieutenant scratched his green hair
as the rattle of wagon wheels drew near.
Too late now for his father to object;
that worthy had gone to search for his son—
the idealized version, not this aspect
who was a bit cracked from seeing black suns
rise ringed by fiery coronas in burnt
siena skies; they resembled black eyes
swallowing the sun's gold light, and they weren't
right; such a sense of wrongness had gripped vise-
tight, clamping down on reason until
none remained. Such a sight he couldn't forget,
not when it telegraphed evil's rise which will
expand, come here to Shayari this threat.
Evil expands daily; what can small men
do when they're tall as boots of larger men?
Chero didn't know, and he wrestled with this
as the cart halted by the Guardian.
He lay in a cleared patch of grass with his
sword at his side battling obsidian night
with its white glow augmented by the red
light of lumir stones that ringed his body.
Had the Undeem's touch and its shadows shred
part of this man's soul or his tall body?
He was five-and-three-quarter times Chero's
height and more than twice that of the Groundlings
lifting him into the cart; reverent though
they stayed, that little group, ne'er a Groundling
said a single word as crystal sword and
man lay blanket-wrapped by a stranger's hands.
The cart turned then, its bed full and its task
only half-done, turned towards that underground

village, sheathed in the sword's glow; will it mask
their presence from the Undeem? Or will sound
give them away? A blue glow flits catching
his eye; it's Anasril trading driver's
bench for a look at him, whom she's saving.
Chero flies, ignores objections offered
by his father's men; she's a puzzle worth
solving and perhaps helping a warrior
of the light will help one day to save th'earth.
He joins Anasril, who is checking for
life; what else can one small warrior do but
lend aid to those who can slash evil's gut?
Anonymous woman, brunette for now,
crosses the One Continent; Shayari's
at her back, before her the west sprawls bowed
down by war prosecuted by no free-
thinking fool; no not this time, not her fight
either, she's seeking the old gods, those brats;
pantheons that disbelief broke, blighted
by mad fools who "never let go of that
passionate drive called desire" even when
common sense should have kicked in and kicked out
such notions; butterflies dance where light dens.
Fallow fields, felled fowls and forests routed
stills her steps in day's bitter washed-out shine.
Mile upon mile, destruction falls in line.
Long grasses wave in the wind combing them.
Scenting ashes and sulfur stink, she sits
to contemplate, her back to a condemned
barn, a burnt-out husk left behind as fit
tribute to lives ill-spent; how long had sleep
turned the season's wheel while flesh and time's cage
hadn't contained her? While she'd walked starry keeps,
rode the lightning streak of time back to ages
when tech ruled, beyond that to god-fearing
times where magic's rooted, sideways through dreams

to Shayari, where in a cave resting,
she'd waited for reasons to break from dreams
and quit talking to bug-eyed aliens,
those rotund, green-skinned Aurelians.
So engaged in her mental haranguing
was she that rising, she began to walk.
Her heart piloted her feet; fears roaring
in her ears, she ran north tearing up stalks
as she used every trick she'd learned to shrink
the distance between here and *there*—an ice
palace where justice's sighs dismiss inked
claimants in that bustling, cadet blue, vice-
(and lice-) -free metropolis sculpted band
by blue-toned band by hands of no prince charmed
or otherwise, though he had won her hand.
For a time, she'd owned a name until harm
threatened those she'd loved; power's price, she'd paid
by becoming nameless and like that she'd stayed.
Landscapes fluctuated 'tween destruction
and verdant forest, then between glacial
sheet and tundra as her transportation
spell, which had a few kinks with its spacial
recognition, dropped her down a shaft soot-
stained and landed her on a hearth's coal bed.
She rose like a revenant and shook soot
from her clothes 'till sight of a frozen head
and a ravaged body slumped on a throne—
all encased in an ice-block three-feet thick—
arrested her; she threw off shock and honed
her magic in on the problem right-quick.
With the Storm King imprisoned, winter raged
unchecked, leaving spring a battle to wage.
"I did warn you about your obsession
with ice," she said unable to resist
a captive audience in possession
of consciousness as his blue eyes insist.

"But what does the Anonymous woman
know? I'm just the wild mage who's rescuing
your frosty butt. What's that? You talking, man?"
His lips moved, but no words passed the roaring
wind that her tinkering kicked up. Some proof
of who'd done this vile deed? Pain speared her mind.
His eyes stole her words, rearranged and poof!
They dropped re-ordered into her shocked mind.
"Maelstrom, runaway," he said with mind's gift,
the one magic that can't be taken by theft...
Henneth woke to a strange sight—a glowing
globe spun in a silver cage suspended
from a mosaic'd sky. Pendulums swing
back and forth—if they fell, they'd squash him dead.
He looked at that light whose shine was sun-like
and yet it didn't blind like the sun's burning
eye; he wond'red why it's white that bright spike.
Why not canary that crystal spinning,
whose strange sight boggles his sleep-muddled mind?
He could bide here awhile while pieces swarm
'bout his mind trying and failing to find
a place in that tenebrous mire where warm
thoughts twist into cold dread and visions passed:
a baby, a dark thing with claws stealing past...
Hen sat up and fought down histrionic's
friend, panic, for the baby they'd taken.
Around him spread a place quite botanic
with Groundlings, if he is not mistaken.
The Little Folk paused leaving carts to block
the flower-lined lanes between their stone homes.
A bubble of blue light bobbed and wove. Shock
made Hen feel faint at the sight of—a gnome?
Two small and butterfly-winged—fairy folk?
She stood eleven inches in bare feet;
her gauzy pink dress, breeze-ruffled like smoke,
hung to her knees; 'side her landed no sweet

38

escort but a lowering storm twelve inches,
boots to crown, a moth-winged prince who didn't flinch.
"You're okay!" squeaked the Anandarwen girl.
Her companion stayed silent and deadly as smoke.
"I'm Anasril, and he's Chero," the girl
continued, giving her dark friend a poke.
He stayed firm as iron and quiet as still air.
No toxicity or hostility,
not in that boyish man with wings, but there's
something about him—a nobility
in those foreign eyes. Eyes that've seen things
that would make Hen shudder if he unlocked
those lips and pulled word from that youth—some things
in ignorance's domain are best locked.
Adapting is for the young in body
not the old and tired who just want to be.
"Did you see a baby?" Hen asked knowing
the answer before two fair faces fell,
and two dark heads shook; neither spoke letting
the silence say what they could not and fell
him with grief's ax at the thought of a babe
taken by dark pow'rs in that savage night.
Chero spoke then, "The Undeem took the babe.
We heard his cry fading into the night."
"You heard but did not see, so you don't know
where they took the child or where I should search?"
'Twas subtle that shift, the firmed spine—he knows,
that Chero; his averted gaze—a lurch
he's in now; for the magical speak true,
if lies they spew, each one they'll live to rue.
A furtive glance at the girl clarifies;
Chero won't speak of what he knows in front
of her, and that means these Undeem, despised
by all, have homes difficult to confront.
A woman with a violet kerchief and gray
hair pulled back arrived amid the grumbling,

holding a bowl of soup on a gilt tray.
She stood three-feet-tall. With a smile jumbled
his thoughts as hunger took o'er, and a crowd
of Groundlings gathered 'round waiting to hear
a tale of heroes, one fitting the proud
blade a-glow by their guest r'minding that queer
creature, Fate had passed near and regarded
then targeted, a life use discarded.
Hen breathed in humid air, and the truth fell
willingly from his lips. "I found the sword.
I'm bound for a city to return—" A bell
rang in warning; hunting horns sounded chords
of dread as they climbed into the clarino
register; their frightful call rose e'en high'r
into octaves he couldn't hear, but Chero
and Anasril kept their ears plugged, then sighed
in relief as the horns passed out of their range.
Through the oculus above the crystal
swinging, night had cloaked the sky and its strange
children, the Undeem, walked as shadow's thralls.
Hen drank the soup, stood with the sword in hand
ready to run and seek the Undeem's lands...
"What the hell's a maelstrom?" Th'Anonymous
woman asked, but her interlocutor's
icy prison prevented speech and that must
have smarted, or perhaps his modular
state accounted for his rolling blue eyes.
Winds whipped her as the roof tore free and rose,
lifted by winds encircling a black eye.
The sun, reduced to a brown mote that rose
centered in that eye; its shine'd burned off; left
a cinder, a spherical splinter in
that sky-swallowing eye that left no cleft
unseen from horizon-to-horizon.
Her thoughts tumbled like wave-tossed shells that fell
on the shores of her mind: Maelstrom, they spelled.

"I figured that out," she said as winds tore
with invisible hands at her own mind.
Letter by letter it snatched the word 'fore
she could find its source and reply in kind.
She'd given up her name but not her pow'r.
"Time to go your frostiness." Shrill chanting
in a dark canon no less, cut off her
monologue with its discordant howling.
Each wail lashed at identity's core, scored
wounds that bled mem'ry and dreams, draining life's
essence, leaving her excoriated
psyche cracked and breaking up as her life,
long-lived, stuttered like a flame almost snuffed.
Bits of her sloughed off; holding on was tough.
But she held on and sought winter's mantle.
Somehow it's tied to that all-consuming
eye and th'evil mind's drive to dismantle.
Her magic's questing, finding snow's cloaking
power and breaking its seal so winter's
ice-crown falls from the Storm King's surprised brow.
Falling, it changes to an owl, winter's
bird-of-choice, and it wings far to crown, now,
a new Storm King and lay the mantle on
another's shoulders thus freeing the deposed
Storm King, her cadet-blue-eyed flame whose gone
quite white; his breaking prison poses
no obstacle now that winter's mantle's
not feeding it; still, they've got a battle.
Ice shards swept up by winds, turn into knives
that spin, slice flesh as they rocket by, turn,
and come again like groups of scorned wives.
More join the first batch and their cold cuts burn
as the ice prison shatters and out falls
the former Storm King; his elemental
magic's gone but his mind, its power falls–
guillotines the maelstrom's purely mental

hold freeing th'Anonymous woman 'fore
her being's frayed beyond recall; pieces
fall now into place, shroud her naked core
and shield it from that swirling eye. Released
her from its stranglehold, sweet relief, bowled
her o'er, made her stagger 'till he caught hold.
"Now'd be a good time to do that translate-
thing and shift us to somewhere friendlier
to life and limb 'fore it makes us blank slates—
enslaved puppets who, to its will, adhere."
Th'Anonymous woman gathered her wits
behind her former husband's mental shields.
She called up her map, added a grid, split
her attention 'tween here and far afield.
She selected a car'bbean green square,
ran its coordinates through equations.
Simple algebra, yes, but she didn't dare
attempt transcontinental-translation
without working it through first, else tragic
things result when bad math mixed with magic.
Coordinate geometry's result
startled her, but she fed it into spells
she'd copied long ago out of a dolt's
second-hand grimoire; she fed pow'r to spells
she'd used to arrive and with a cry, for
she'd not thought to scry, the spell grabbed her waist
and flung her and Istan across space; for
she'd forgotten to account, in her haste,
for the planet's curvature! So they sped
like thrown balls that gravity snagged and dragged
dirt-wards at high velocity with dread.
She'd many magical tricks but none tagged
for such a problem. But on the fly, try
she did. Their fall slowed; with relief, she sighed.
Undreal hid from day's flaxen rays that streamed
gold filaments through the forest's leaf-roof.

Its touch burned her in her burrow; tears streamed
down her shadowed face and kissed the babe, proof
in her arms that she was no demon maid.
Fumbling fingers located her tarot
deck; she drew them out, shuffled them afraid
to find out if Fate would throw future woes
her way. Cold cards slide against her palm—draw
one and risk it or put it back unseen?
She'd hours to fill before night broke the thaw
and cold descended deep, without star's gleam.
Moon-dark nights are best for hunting mortals;
'cept the Undeem hunt her from their portals.
Renegade—a state she'd attained through mercy,
a crime among the Undeem, and this child-
she'd aided anchored her to controv'rsy,
to this plane and made vuln'rable a wild
thing unused to responsibility.
She cowered from sun's fire and drew a card;
the Empress stared back at her, the guilty
one; her finger traced the cerise gown; card's
faded from long ownership, which muted
the colors, but not its heavy portent.
Motherhood, mother earth—meanings rooted
in the continuance of this farce, meant
to end her and the child when the fight came.
No way could she fight a horde that became.
Day disappeared into hushed misery.
Night fell, and the Undeem's trackers sifted
scents carried by wind, seeking not faery
blood but mortal child; hunting calls drifted;
they made no secret of their search; no need
for stealth when they'd thousands, and she's alone.
From her mossy bed, she rose, swayed, she'd feed
later. Now's for running because night's thrown
her no bone by hiding moon's light, making
it easier for the Undeem to hunt.

They see best in deepest darkness, needing
no light at all, nor does she, streaking front
and center, hiding won't help, running might,
anything to postpone a losing fight.
Holding the babe tight, she runs, becoming
a breath of wind rustling the leaves; not fast
enough, they're gaining; their horns are calling
their beasts to the chase. Trees stand as the last
barrier—those enchanted witnesses,
they don't help her; their bark eyes look away
as yipping hordes ripple from their synthesis,
sent by their mistress, the Empress, whose way
is never thwarted, the bitch goddess, night's
ruler and the Undeem's too; surrounded,
Undreal's turning, keeping her charge from sight.
Shapes morph from the formless cloth of the dead
of night; they rush her, hit her with their spells—
incantations she's able to repel.
Realizing their error, they tag-team, throw
punches she dodges, but there's too many.
Grasping hands catch her, allowing more blows
to land 'till she's curled about the baby,
protecting its carnation cheeks, its pale
skin and its little limbs from harm; intact,
he'll stay for how long, she can't say; she's failed.
They're going back to the Undeem's lands, a fact
that makes her sick with dread; action ceases,
they've trussed her up with invisible bonds.
She can't escape or move 'cept in pieces.
Carry her back and the child too; still fond
she is of this one who caused her to break
free, and in her hands, her unlife, she takes.
Swift the horde moves, flowing over hill, dale
and valley, streaming between trees, fleeing
coming dawn, whose singing her swan song; pale
sparks it sends up to light the clouds reeling

from night's departure, not quick 'nough to save
her, and that makes her laugh; delirium's
settling in since she hasn't fed; no life caved
to hunger; insanity's atrium
beckoned, but a wail recalled her senses.
She had lived a mortal's life for two days
with fierce determination; defenses
'gainst a hunger, the babe could've sated, stayed.
She'd cared for the child, tucked deep in shadow,
and she'd felt peace root in her heart and grow.
The Undeem roil like a black-faceless tide.
An ebb and flow of shadow she'd once known,
embraced as truth 'cause all things fade; deride
death if you must, but its henchmen aren't drones.
They loathe human life, human flesh, solid-
bone cages where resides a soulful treat—
and she's one of them, hunger made solid,
shadow given woman's seeming, where beat
no heart. She's animated by unlife.
Undreal's a daughter of th'Undeem horde, now
sorry not for what she lost, but the life
she might have spent, but that life's as lost now
as that kidnapped baby. He's not her own;
her love for him has grown and dissent sown.
None of the Undeem touched that child, carried
in her bound arms, he cried, and his tears soaked
her form; their strange wetness somehow married
her to corporeality and coaxed
her true form back from the Undeem's ether
preventing her from merging and losing
herself to undiff'rentiation; her
will's not subl'mated to th'Empress' bidding,
not this time, not this rebellion in tears
flowing anew as the Undeem dive down
through frigid water to the sunken smear
that resolves into a daisy-shaped town--

a city whose name history has swept
away; its ghosts, for that injustice wept.
Down they poured through crack and crevice, weaving
around columns that hold roofs up no more
to the Empress' hall, where they're tossing
her down on cold tiles free of water's war
to destroy this place; best of luck she wishes
to that downpour widening the crack above.
Let it drown this place, make th'Undeem fishes
instead of fishers of men who gut their loves
and pull out their souls, adding their conquests
to the horde until pity elicits
a choice—wish it'd deaden fears in her breast.
The Empress' claw extends to solicit
an explanation, but Undreal has none,
It was pity that made her come undone.
Now she lay unable to move, like prey,
like the human adversary without
a cross or symbol of creation's say
in these matters, nor belief just her doubts
and an irrelevant desire to know
what could have been if she'd escaped and raised
the child pity made her hold, who lay so
cold, wet and wailing in misery's haze.
Nothing could she do to ease or delay
her fate or the child's; 'twas the Empress' whim
that would hold sway; that burned and made her fey.
Made her struggle against formless bonds, half-
here and on other planes; the Empress laughed.
The Empress leaned in, her hibiscus-kissed
lips breathing in fear and anger; savor
them, she does. So rare a gift from child-missed
to thing forgotten, twisted from favor
of demons into shadow creatures, bland
puppets whose unlife makes the Creator
squirm; by choice they came to her ranks to stand

in her cerulean realm to serve. They swore
attrition of the human herd by choice,
by her grand design now foiled by this one
wretched thing, who'd half-reversed the change choice'd
made and for what? A squalling babe? That one's
better of as fish food; its soul's too small
to feed her; what good is his life at all?
The Groundlings rushed to discover the source
of the horn calls, and what new danger shrilled
its challenge into the night; Henneth's course
was set, he'd a babe to locate; he'd kill
the Undeem. They'd interfered with his plan.
He needed a location from Chero.
His girl fluttered o'er to see how things stand.
Intercepting the black, moth-winged Chero
before he could follow the migration
to th'other side of the cavern where ramps
led up and out, Henneth put his question
to the scamp to loosen the info clamped.
"Where's the Undeem's lair? Who's their cynosure?
He'll want a ransom for the babe, I'm sure."
Chero wrestled with th'answer and tried on
and rejected, the idea of keeping
quiet, 'till compassion, his battle won.
"You'll need a submersible for this thing."
Henneth ignored that; the word meant nothing.
He hefted his scrip, hoped those horns meant no
harm and nodded for Chero to take wing.
"There a back out of here? Do you know?"
Chero pointed to the bright pendulum
in its wire cage suspended o'er the cave.
Henneth looked at the nice ramp feeling glum;
he withdrew a rope to climb like a knave.
Chero took the end, carried it aloft,
tied a knot and signaled Hen to be off.
Hen felt each of his five-plus-decades pile-

drive him into exhaustion as he climbed.
Yet reach the oculus 'neath which that phial
of brilliant light swung he did, and he timed
his ungainly exit to coincide
with the returning tread of the Groundlings.
The moonless night caressed his heaving side
as he lay gasping then up he's moving.
He'd wasted enough time since the babe's loss.
E'ery sinew was tired, but he started
off signaling his moth-winged guide to cross
into uncharted forest; they parted
ways with the light-filled world of rescuers
heading to a land where nightmares skewer...
Melanin blended Chero's wings with night.
Henneth wondered if that adaptation
developed to help hide him from th'Undeem's sight.
He didn't ask as miles piled up and action
neared; Hen stopped when the sun struck gold melting
night into nickel-plated dawn over
a lake whose spoon shaped embankment, a thing
not of sand but of rocks smoothed by water.
"They're down there with the kelp aren't they?" Hen sighed
at Chero's nod, 'course the feckin' Undeem
were a pelagic folk, and he couldn't bide
here to wait for them to surface; it seemed
a cold swim in water dawn-painted blue
was inevitable, which he would rue.
"The lake's bed runs deep enough that no sun
ever touches it," Chero replied with
a nonchalant shrug he didn't feel while one
step away from the lair of death's cruel smith.
Chero shuddered and rose on beating wings
'till he clawed the sky high above the nut-
branches to see what he'd dreaded: winging
like a blue arrow 'gainst the raw morn—what
he'd hoped to avoid, Anasril, who'd come

to join them on phase two of this quest; but
how'd she track them? She hovered and struck dumb
by this deviation from plan, he said,
"they'll mutilate us both and make us dead."
Horn calls sounded in the distance and made
them look to the horizon for answers.
They saw none as they drifted on wind's blade
that riled the trees on shore, and their green fur.
"It's a party of men. That's what I came
to tell you. They're hunting some organic
thing—some herb that flowers by night and tames
fevers and panic with charms-botanic."
Anasril's frank gaze declared that reason
an excuse and a lucky one for them.
Perhaps more than three would storm th'Undeem's sun-
less bolt hole, adding more to be condemned.
He nodded, and they dropped down to explain
to Henneth about help defeating life's bane.

To be continued.

BETH PATTERSON

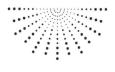

BIOGRAPHY

Beth W. Patterson was a full-time musician for over two decades before diving into the world of writing, a process she describes as "fleeing the circus to join the zoo". She is the author of the books *Mongrels and Misfits, The Wild Harmonic,* and a contributing writer to twenty anthologies.

Patterson has performed in eighteen countries across the Americas, Europe, Oceania, and Asia. Her playing appears on over a hundred and seventy albums, soundtracks, videos, commercials, and voice-overs (including seven solo albums of her own). More than a hundred of her compositions and co-writes have been released. She studied ethnomusicology at University College, Cork in Ireland and holds a Bachelor's degree in Music Therapy from Loyola University New Orleans.

Beth has occasionally worn other hats as a body paint model, film extra, minor role actor, recording studio partner, record label owner, producer, and visual artist. She is a lover of exquisitely stupid movies and a shameless fangirl of the band Rush. Visit her website for more information.

ANXIETY DREAM

Above the crowd's chaotic din
The surge of bodies pressing in
I walk the plank to where my fear awaits

The magistrate is void and null
But grinning like an empty skull
The verdict just a list of loves and hates

A cleft dividing foe and friends
The gavel's solid blow descends
My solace repossessed, a swift farewell

Oh foolish judge, just let it be
You cannot get the best of me
I'll spit at you beyond the gates of hell!

MINOTAUR

Where did my predatory instinct go?
It's not the sort of thing that one discards
The greatest challenge splintered into shards
A tiresome and time-consuming foe

Why did suspicion choose another friend?
My mind was once its favorite place to dwell
Not even brash authorities can tell
Their expert tongues no longer condescend

How did I come to quickly find the key?
The winding thread, my footsteps to retrace
The labyrinth, the beast I had to face
And realize the Minotaur was me

And now each phantom crumbles into dust
And every nightmare safely filed away
My heart can sleep among the dreams at play
The day a troubled creature learns to trust

When peace has heard my every crime confessed
She wraps me in her arms and bids me rest

YARD SALE

"Why would a person want this gift?
If I received it, I'd be miffed.
This angel looks like Frankenstein
I'd keep it hidden were it mine!
Lopsided features lacking trust,
The twisted metal laced with rust,
The heart is gone, the wretched soul,
And look, the wings are full of holes!
That freak would never leave the ground."
(And so she put the mirror down.)

PAPER

Afraid of paper tigers
Shot down by paper planes
While writing down a wish made on
A thousand paper cranes

Though sticks and stones can hurt you
Bad news can rip your guts
One letter can destroy you with
A thousand paper cuts

NO SUCH THING

Exposing every foible, and even loved for this
The strength to shed my armor, raw emotion, finding bliss
A crossing of two journeys that I never could forget
"There's no such thing," I told myself
And yet
And yet

The value of my laughter past the price of every song
A comfort zone in heaven where I finally belong
A night of wine and vinyl and a little red Corvette
"There's no such thing," I told myself
And yet
And yet

Warm skin and supple muscle, breath of life and solid bone
My fingers trace a wordless secret language of our own
The polyrhythms of our hearts my favorite duet
"It's real," I do believe I said
Well met
Well met

SPACES

If I wish for guidance
Of events yet to be seen
I look not to constellations
But the spaces in between

For the stars have been long dead
By the time our faces warmed
The greatest premonitions
Are in stars yet to be formed

EVEN

They say an eye for an eye
Is a tactic base and vicious
"Don't sink to that same level!"
But oh, gods! It's so delicious!

RED FLAGS

What instinct comes to mind
When the red haze hits the public
Where arrows fly and tender hearts are pierced?

I make myself go small
To hide from all my flaws
Roiled by angry voices harsh and fierce

I'm a scapegoat, I'm a burden
I'm a waste of time and space
Thought I've never asked a boon in all my life

Most see nights of wine and chocolate
Rosy petals, precious gems
Cherub's arrows, but I only see a knife

VOLITION

I am largely comprised of odd meter and storms
Of primeval flames and black smoke descending
But this heart that slams against its iron cage
Will never desert you

My diet consists of lightning and fables
With a side of chaos and latent longing for dessert
But I would eat my fears alive
To keep you by my side

I slake my thirst on desert rain
Dreamless sleep and hidden countermelodies
But if you offered me a cup of mystery to be continued
I would drink without hesitation
And might never again fear the dark

SUSPEND

Crosshairs divided
Still wholly undecided
Resolute, remorseful
Determined and resourceful
Emphatic, erratic
With a flair for the dramatic
I will bait you, await you
And try hard not to hate you

NICE

You know it's because she loves you
That she builds you a nice safe cage
A nice normal life to rot you
With other nice kids your age

No herald to open a window
And ceilings on all your ideals
No one to hold you close nightly
For she knows all too well how that feels

RESTLESS

Sometimes my sleep is restless, with old yearnings too involved
Within my dreams a war between redemption and resolve
And with a pang I call my waking mind to intervene
So is it any wonder that I chug so much caffeine?

EDGE

"You're an odd one," said the blacksmith
"But as per your strange request,
I have customized your sword to single-edged

One side can never hurt you
And the other slays your foe
But there's still a disadvantage," he alleged

"Your beloved's less at risk
But you are vulnerable now
And the cutting edge holds just as sharp a sting

I suppose I should remind you
For a hundred reasons hence
That you must be careful where you point that thing!"

A GIANT'S CAUSE

Ever since the incident, I've been wrong in the head.
"But you're the great Goliath!" the astonished doctor said.
"Now get back on that battlefield, your minions to employ!"
You'll never know just how a tiny pebble can destroy.

FULL CIRCLE

Uncounted years ago
He steered me from my course
But when I faltered in the race
He backed another horse

Unnumbered times since then
He broke the cosmic laws
With many faces, trickster god
Who ridiculed my flaws

We come full circle now
A denouement delayed
Will history repeat itself?
Step forth and taste my blade

REMORSE

A hero's return to redemption
Is not for the weak or faint-hearted
"X" marks the spot in the center
A map I too quickly discarded
So riddle me this: were it valid,
Then where would I even have started?

MARK

Anyone can suffer ink and needles
Such covenant can only go skin deep
For even with a rite of pain and bloodshed
A mark is just a mark and talk is cheap

The ink upon a treaty is a gesture
And proof of fealty is just abstraction
But when the flesh has aged and parchment crumbled
My lasting testimony will be action

STONES

I declare it's for the birds
Regarding sticks and stones and words
For there's damage to be done with threats and lying

Though I vow I won't be haunted
When I'm ridiculed and taunted
For fuck's sake, I really wish they would stop trying

BARGAIN

Don't tamper with the dark arts that you borrow from your muse
Unless you let the swamp sing in your blood
And don't unlock the floodgates you pretend you don't abuse
I know that you cannot survive a flood

If you choose to romanticize an art that's born from pain
You pay with disillusionment for dues
I'll take away each comfort until only fears remain
You got your wish, and now you sing the blues

SHOCK

Don't reignite with matches
A hollow heart gone blind
Just sit with me in shadows
Until I change my mind

BONES

The past is a backward-flowing river
With a current that will forever defeat me
Drowning me in mockery alleged to be an illusion
And depositing what remains of me in the riverbed

So I will let my own darkness rise and hide my bones
Until my existence is reduced to a rumor
And my words an obsolete farmer's almanac

There is no future in preserving sentiment
All recorded facts point to this

EPILOGUE

The low man on the totem pole in heaven
The monarch of the empty room in hell
And which man had the better of those outcomes?
Empty shell
Empty shell

My tail goes in my mouth, and I say nothing
The poison in my blood leaves every cell
As springtime turns to summer's mad perspective
Time will tell
Time will tell

The bulwark of my thoughts a pile of rubble
To sensible I bid a coarse farewell
The humming of my nerves in seven octaves
All is well
All is well

HAIKUS

"Are you born again?"
"I suppose," I said at last
"Just not how you want."

Burned-out shotgun shell
Still warm in the aftermath
Sees no road ahead

Some folks seem to think
That I can't feel love or pain
That's showbiz, I guess

Sometimes I'm afraid
She could kill me with a word
Still I stand my ground

This is just a test
Spread my tongue, clamp down my teeth
Reflexes remain

Perception is odd
When I hear in black and white
Color floods my mind

SOFI LAPORTE

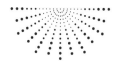

Sofi Laporte was born in Austria, grew up in Korea, studied Comparative Literature in the USA, and lived in Ecuador with her Ecuadorian husband. When not writing, she likes to scramble about the beautiful Austrian country side exploring medieval castle ruins. She currently lives with her husband, three trilingual children, and a cat in Upper Austria.

RODIN'S KISS

One long finger trails along the shivering
arch glistening with inner pulsating
light exploding in iridescent
whiteness, soft and moist
it trails, the muscles flex, a
compressed taut grip
surrendered and lost in a jumble
of billowing strands and
silken light
an eye-lash kiss of feather
shadows and sweat pearls
roll along the pliant, soft
curves, buried in eternity
molten and frozen in one
chip of milky marble.

(inspired by the sculpture *The Kiss* by Auguste Rodin in the Rodin
Museum, Paris).

EMBROIDERED BY TIME

Cast a net of memories
spun by time-threads
silvery-fine

love flies away
hope blanches with time
memory alone preserves
dreams for a while

time-threads weave dreams
of crystals and gold
light breaks the crystals
iridescently bold

the gold is for smiled
the crystals for tears
the rainbows for triumph
of love over fear

if it must be
then let love fly

then loosen the threads
silvery-fine

tears that fall are
embroidered by time
let memories preserve
dreams for a while.

BOY EYES

I see boy eyes
of a melting husky brown
sweet & wild
they caress gently
gleam & glide
up my neck &
down my breast
provoking wild
twinkling in a naughty light
you have such soul eyes
open wide
of a melting husky brown
sweet & wild
kissing & kissing & kissing
so
why why why
cant you own
the truth that's in your eyes

LOVING DUST

Luscious scraps are scattered everywhere
I crawl on my knees and gather
them together, weeping.
Splinters, fragments, particles of dust
sweet dust, loving dust
merge with my tears.
My face smeared with tears and
arms filled with loving dust and
fragments and splinters
I say, defiantly:
It was never wrong.

DOLLY

There lies my dolly
dusty-eyed
joints are rusted
lace yellow-dyed
one eye-lid is stuck
the seam torn wide
cotton filling is
spilling out of one side

There lies my dolly
crumpled, dried
often coddled, dropped
and flung
to the side
many a secret
patient to hide
of a willful child
dreaming of being
a radiant bride

There lies my dolly

left to abide
powdery patched
porcelain white
forevermore smiling
and smiling
though time took
a stride –
last glimmer
of magic has flickered
and died.

WOMANHOOD

I've seen her before, beneath the tree,
more often sitting on the swing,
with swirling hair and brimful,
dreamy eyes.
She looked at me and laughed,
her head thrown back to show
her long, clean throat
she said but "come"
but I did not.

I bit my braids in anguish
then turned – looked back,
but she was gone.

At times I'd see her sit or stand
in corners, aisles or streets, more
often by the swing
so that I dared not use it anymore.

Sometimes she'd beckon with one hand
reach out one curvy arm, and once I

nearly touched her with my pudgy finger
then pulled back swiftly lest she grabbed me
hard and wouldn't let go.

I threw my braids back in defiance and cried "NO!"
How I would claw and scratch and bite if she but
dared to touch me!

Then I saw the sadness in her eyes
she disappeared and no more did she sit upon my swing
and I was glad.

One day I stood before the mirror
with my braids undone, and she stared
right back at me
with brimful eyes and swirling hair.
Aghast, she looked, and shook her head
then smiled – forgot to braid her hair
and left to sit and ponder on the swing.

MOONWOMAN

Weeping wildly
I pressed my face into the grass
when she came
silently from behind
with the silent rustle
of her blue-green silk
she took my face firmly
between her hands and I looked
into her eyes and saw
the moonwoman
gaze back at me with eyes big,
innocent, with endless wisdom,
ancient knowledge, a priestess
of the stars.

MELODY OF THE SOUL

My melody winds itself into
a vortex of fibrous substance
not at all tangible. Maybe it'll
dissolve into puff one day
leaving silver glitter like
star dust of a
lost generation.

With no Armageddon ever.

Sometimes the melody slushes
in a tiresome swirl restlessly
romping like brazen children
refusing to take their naps.
how annoying.

Then it's more like silence,
rather, a holy hush refusing
to be heard.
I always knew my melody was different.

No melody's the same
his has no tunes at all
for me to hear, merely a metallic
clank of tin boxes scraping
on concrete or like sharp
knives etching into glass,
squeaking and screaking coldly
A goospimply sound.

It hurts my ears though I don't
hear it, of course, but his eyes
aglaze speak of it and his
twisted mouth utters its
clamor. I shiver

Let it not overtune my Melody
let there be no Armageddon.

Only when he is gone I hear my
melody again
quietly murmuring
then culminating in a symphony
of triumphing echoes.

M E

Beneath torrents exploding in colourless
black and
fata Morganas blinding
the eye with hysterical colour
and vain wishes, false
identities, death-games
and vampirical laughs
sneering at a mask without a face
there is a quiet source of
unimaginable gentleness
defying with a loving chuckle
the caricature
which is not me.

QUINTESSENCE

It is possible to feel the moon.
It has cool fingers.
They glide over my skin and color it
creamy.
It is possible to feel the moon.
Its breath is warm with absorbed
mortal glances and mortal thoughts
century-old with suffering.
Do not reject me, it whispers, it begs.
I can teach you loneliness.

LADY OF THE WINDS

I saw at first a flicker of her dress
beneath the gloomy shadows of the trees
and then a silver sheen
her silken hair spread wide
in subtle waves
her icy pouting lips with hesitancy
brushed my cheeks – I felt
the warmness drain from them
and paralyzing coldness swept through the
chambers of my heart – what immortality!
I longed to be with her, the silver maid
to fly with her and caress all the trees
the hills the plains and tempt the
tranquil waters to rebel…
I looked into her face – and then
I stood alone beneath the trees.

TERRY MILLER

BIOGRAPHY

Terry Miller lives in Portsmouth, Ohio. His work has been featured in Sanitarium, Devolution Z, the 2017 Rhysling Anthology, Poetry Quarterly, O Unholy Night in Deathlehem Anthology, The Horror Tree's Trembling With Fear, and Jitter Press. Upcoming anthologies scheduled for release in 2019 are set to feature his poetry and stories as well. Miller prefers to write horror but has branched out a bit to include Science Fiction, though still with a horror slant, and a diverse poetic voice. He hopes to complete his first novella, as well as continue to contribute to magazines and anthologies, by the end of this year. You can find him on Facebook here:

facebook.com/tmiller2015/

BREATHE FOR A MOMENT

Life is a freight train, let me off
I want to dive inside a storybook
Where I can mark my page, walk away,
And breathe for a moment.
Life is a sad place, let me go
Infinite worlds await, you see
And I can mark my page, walk away
To breathe for a moment.
Life is a nightmare, wake me up
A story I read may be too much
But I can mark my page, walk away,
And breathe for a moment.

UNTITLED

Put on a face, don't let them see;
After all, the whole world's a masquerade.
Shakespeare had it right, this is a stage,
All you see, all there is
A society of plastic people playing their roles.
When will the curtain close, aren't you sick of pretending?
Yourself defending, amending your speech etiquette,
Treading these eggshells lest we offend,
Lest we show people who we are,
Lest we don't live by someone else's ideals.
God forbid someone is made to love us for us and not some general
semblance.
So what if you cry?
So what if you shut down 'cause this world's too much?!
So what if you're angry, or for one moment, just one,
You take some time to breathe.
Forgive us heaven, or forgive us hell,
For this script we've been given is shit!

ECHOES

I've laid down the hate
Yet the anger remains
Your words, they echo
They resonate
They penetrate, they've penetrated
And embedded, my psyche - fractured
This is what I've become
A vapor, a stain,
A shell of a man, myself an echo
In some hallowed hall
That once housed your pedestal
It's dim, the light seldom shines
Our conversations dwell,
A turntable in my ear
Spins, keeps spinning
Forever for me to hear
This is my prison,
What was my crime?

THE MOCKERY

My love, how have you grown so pale?
In the moonlight, even the owl questions who you've become!
These tiring hours boast no conclusions,
And the ticking clock is but a mockery!
How dire is this circumstance,
How deep your desire!
With such shallow breaths your chest does heave,
And the death in your eyes still gazes a beckoning stare
Into the night where the creatures roam.
My love, how have you grown so cold?
In the moonlight, your lips glow a luminescent blue!
These trying hours host my confusion,
And the ticking clock is but a mockery!
How strange is this spectacle!
How disturbing your eye!
With such shallow depths your soul does leave,
And the breath in your lungs stills with movement bare
As the night echoes a summoning song.
My love, how have you grown so distant?
In the moonlight, the forest winds so tease my ear!
These passing nights, I succumb to madness,

And the ticking clock is but a mockery!
How frail are these mourning bones,
How weak this aching heart!
With such hollow words, I lift my prayers,
And my faith, but a shadow, grows weaker still
As the nights break a man forlorn.
My love, how have you grown so callous?
In the moonlight, you've danced beneath our open window!
The quiet nights erupting with bestial song,
And the ticking clock is but a mockery!
How sorrowful you gaze upon me.
How yearning my gaze returns.
With such fervor is my surrender,
And your touch is frozen with piercing fang
As the veil between worlds is torn!

WE ARE

Of all the things in life we gain,
What of those we lose?
From our first breath,
Fresh out the womb,
It all begins.
If our breaths are numbered,
What is life but a slow death?
This life hosts such heartache.
We love, we lose, we lose more,
For bits of ourselves wither, decay.
We're left an ever-decreasing fraction
Of who we are.

Of all the things in life we choose,
How we acquire those unchosen!
For all we desire,
All our hearts covet,
We're left empty.
Are we that undeserving,
Are we that insignificant,

That we're plagued with such heartache?
We love, we lose, we lose more
For bits of ourselves wither, decay.
We're left an ever-dying creation,
That's what we are.

SEALED WITH A KISS

I remember well and fondly
My own perceptions of love
Before I'd loved.
What it was, what it is, and
What it should be.
A picture perfect expectation,
Both nurturing and true.
A plague of naivety, it was,
And I'm in the aftermath.
This reality, a nightmare,
Dreamt on a bed of lies;
A surprise package, addressed
And sealed with a stranger's kiss.

ANXIETY

Memories creep, they slither
Stalking serpents, venomous
Breaths labored, I wither,
I suffocate, I withdraw
Tongue froze, stutters, lips quiver
Nervous sweat shines, limbs shake, quake
Mind frozen still, delivers
Nothing. Nothing. I'm nothing.

SALOME'S NEW KING

In the darkness, where she dwells, her breath is on my skin.
Her nails pierce the flesh, her voice provokes a thousand sins.
She prays unto some unknown god, words I dare not to recite,
As she comes from the shadows that blend into the dreadful night.

Her silhouette upon the wall, and quiet footsteps on the floor.
Her legs soon drape to either side, I am her fleshling whore.
Paralyzed and short of breath with hands upon my throat,
My heart feels crushed beneath the weight of hate and shattered hope.

Whispers from her lips seem locked in monotonous chant.
Her body bends, contorts, and morphs into some awkward slant.
Consciousness evades me as her form continues to writhe,
A netherworld surrounds me, it and reality collide.

Pain and ecstasy are one where realms begin to weave.
My lungs take in sulfuric ash, it makes it hard to breathe.
Her ember eyes burn with fire, piercing into my soul,
Then dim into an empty stare till both are black as coal.

They draw me into the dark, into some vast abyss.

Death is there to greet me floating upon the River Styx.
His boney hand points the way, we sail toward the land
Of fire and ash, of serpents' tongues, and evil's grave demands.

She greets me there, the barren land, that rootless, blackened soil.
Upon the shoreline, the river's red and waters heat to boil.
The skyline's painted crimson and distant ground's set aflame.
She leads me through the burning earth, dust to dust reclaimed.

Her lips spit malicious venom, her mouth speaks, "Follow me."
She is the great seductress, the beautiful Salome.
Dancing like the flames to the beat of tribal drums,
Devils gather in her name, one by one they come.

A wasteland of forgotten lore, all manner of beings dwell.
Abominations procreate things I dare to never tell.
Salome, she takes my hand, and leans in for a kiss.
Poison soon infects my veins, I hear the serpent's hiss.

Her scaly skin pressed to mine, I see her truest form.
Every devil, every beast, they all begin to swarm.
Her claws rip deep, her teeth sink in, I bleed into the earth.
All hail the King, the chosen mate, this is my rebirth.

A CRESCENT MOON STILL SHINES

Towering trees, fluttering leaves,
Branches sway in Autumn breeze
The night is dark, still it breathes
And a crescent moon still shines.

The night wolf sleeps, its hunger grows
The same heart beats, cursed blood flows
A slumber deep, lycans stay low
While a crescent moon still shines.

Mother Earth calls, rise my dear beasts
She sees you're weak, child, come now feast
The strength of most come to the least
As a crescent moon still shines.

Young wolves gather, let forth your howl
Let him question, that curious owl
Who comes now, who comes now
While a crescent moon still shines?

LOVE

Love is an autumn array of color,
A warm breeze on a winter's day.
Love is a flower in bloom and the
Early morning sound of birds in song.
Love is a rainbow after the storm,
The warmth of sunlight on exposed skin.
Love is a river with its twists and turns,
It is land with mountains high and valleys low.
Love is a clear blue sky which sometimes gives
Way to threatening, gray clouds.
Love is trickling streams feeding rivers
In a cycle designed to replenish.
Love is a soft caress from a gentle hand,
The scent of perfume on a pillow.
Love is a shy glance from beneath lashes,
The taste of a kiss from smooth, glossed lips.
And on the days when you find yourself alone,
Love is but a ghost in your arms.

EMPTY SPACES

Every night that I cried for you,
A piece of me washed away.
The innocence of love evaporated
Up to the heavens,
Leaving behind empty spaces.

ONCE

The arms that once held you
Become those which push you away.
The lips that once kissed you
Become the ones that tell lies.
The eyes in which you once stared
Become those of a stranger.
This is love, this is life,
Once, twice, endlessly.

THE WITHERING WOMAN

I awoke to the sound of birds chirping in the hollow,
Peer outside my window to gaze upon a swallow.
The sky clearing to reveal a gentle shade of blue
Brightening with the rising sun, such a comforting hue.
I rise to start my day, the TV blaring down the hall.
I walk into the room and shuttered at what I saw.
There in the corner with a gash on its head.
A body lay motionless, no doubt she was dead.
Empty bottles on the floor, no one died of thirst.
Not another person around, a suspect I was first.
So I buried the body out back in the woods,
Packed the last mound of dirt down best that I could.
I returned to my home to proceed with my shower
And arrived late at work, nine o'clock was the hour.
All day I was quiet, not too productive was I,
Conscience steadily creeping, hungover, my mouth was dry.
I punched the clock and returned to my quaint, quiet house;
Discovered her shirt, buttons torn from the blouse.
Such a sweet smell of honeysuckles I took in with a breath.
I searched all around for anything else I had left.
Now all evidence was gone the best that I knew.

I sat down with a beer and cigarette smoke I blew.
My mind raced for memories, but I could not recall
No bits, no pieces, no recollections at all.
Who was this woman? How I wish I could tell
How she'd come to my door, or how she'd died as well!
What happened in-between to the point of injury?
I entertained the fantasy, such a morbid curiosity!
Another beer from the fridge, ashes falling to the tray,
I twist off the top to let it rest where it lay.
The silence of the house made loud ticks of the clock.
I had a few drinks down when came the faint knock.
Rain was pouring outside, she stood naked and shivering.
Mud covered her feet and her blue lips were quivering.
Without thought I took her in, as pretty as she was.
Her skin was wet and pale, a bit shriveled as water does.
Honeysuckles still seemed fresh on her neck, the sweet scent.
Her body was cold, soft to the touch, and we spent
Hours beneath the covers; her body never seemed to warm.
I paid little mind as we made love into the morn.
Sleep fell upon me but I awoke again to the chirping.
The TV was blaring and my head was hurting.
I walked into the room and just as before,
There her body lay still and naked on the floor!
The cut on her head bled as if it was yet fresh.
Blood trickling down to a stream on her breast.
Was I mad? I pondered but quickly resumed
To carry her to the place her own self she exhumed.
That day was so long as many others I did wait
To repeat the horror of lust we both did satiate.
I lost interest the more she reduced to bones,
Ignored the knocking met with haunting moans.
I awoke one night, her bones rattling my door.
They slowly came louder, I could no longer ignore.
She stood there smiling or, at least, it seemed
For all the flesh was gone, just a skeleton I'd seen.
An arm reached out to clutch my chest,

Digging deeper where my heart did rest.
It was then she tore it from its cage, still beating.
I fell to my knees in the pool I was bleeding.
Death lured me to my cold, quiet grave
In a place beside her own, for me, she had saved.
My own flesh was rotting, my vanity withered.
Bugs came crawling and the worms, they did slither.
A frigid, boney hand soon crept into my own.
We rested there silent until bone was on bone.

DEBBIE MANBER KUPFER

BIOGRAPHY

Debbie Manber Kupfer grew up in the London. She has lived in Israel, New York and North Carolina and somehow ended up in St. Louis. She lives with her husband, two children and two very opinionated felines.

She works as a writer, editor, and a freelance puzzle constructor of word puzzles and logic problems. She is the author of the young adult fantasy series, *P.A.W.S.* which features a secret international organization of shapeshifters. She has also written several children's picture books including *Adana the Earth Dragon* and *Esmeralda Grunch and the Red Tulip*. She is the editor of the *Sins of Time* horror series and has stories in several anthologies including *Fauxpocalypse*, *13 Candles*, *Stardust*, *Always*, *Winter Wishes*, and *Shades of Fear*. She believes that with enough tea and dark chocolate, you can achieve anything!

AT THE DOOR

"Let me in! Let me in! There's a monster out here.
He is ten-foot tall with shaggy green fur
and long sharp claws.
He has one huge purple eye that's staring at me
and rows and rows of pointed teeth
waiting to crunch my bones for his lunch.

He's getting closer. I feel his breath on my neck.
He's licking his lips. He's reaching for me
with his terrible claws.
For the love of all that's holy please let me in!"

Slowly the door creaks open and a face peers out.
"Ah, so he looks just like me, then?"

FIRST CUP OF TEA

I sip from my tea cup
I stare at the page
The world unfolds slowly
The birds take the stage
They circle the trees
But they're scared to embark
The world high above them
Is dangerously dark
The clouds part their ways
As I finish my cup
To find some more words
I will have to wake up.

THE MENACING STORM

The Menacing Storm came rolling in.
"Ha, Ha!" he screamed, "I'll get you all now.
Wet, you will be. Soaked to the skin.
And all because you did not beware,
and pay me some homage and offer a prayer.
Let your umbrellas break,
Let your road be a lake,
Let my thunder and lightning keep you awake."

"Why are you so mean?" asked a brave little cloud.
"I'm not mean," laughed the storm
And he roared to the crowd.
And the rain pelted down all over the town
Until the Menacing Storm at last he said,
"I've had enough now, I'm going to bed!"

ADITYA DESHMUKH

BIOGRAPHY

Aditya Deshmukh is a mechanical engineering student who likes exploring the mechanics of writing as much as he likes tinkering with machines. He writes dark fiction and poetry. He is published in over two dozen anthologies and has a poetry book "Opium Hearts" coming out in June, 2019. He likes chatting with others who share similar interests, so feel free to check him out here too.

REIGN

Eighteen years of captivity had gone,
And still refused Queen Elizabeth to set the Scottish Queen free.
Was a powerless woman, broken and forlorn,
So hard to read?

Accused of her husband's murder,
Separated from her only son,
Robbed of her kingdom by political abusers,
Was she a threat or simply a woman undone?

A tear trickled down Queen Mary's cheek
As she dipped her quill in ink bleak.
She looked at the letter with eyes meek.
Would this letter do the trick?
Or to melt Elizabeth's frozen heart,
The ink, her tears, was too weak?

As days turned into weeks, Mary found it hard to cope.
There was not a glimmer of hope,
because Elizabeth's answer never came;
And Mary felt her spirit wane.

Why was she still a captive?
Why couldn't Elizabeth accept her as a cousin, and not some threat?
Why was she so stubborn, why couldn't she change?
Why wouldn't the storm of their enmity abate?

Gone were the days when Mary considered England hers.
Gone was her curse of ambition that rained embers on her.
Now she was a queen no more,
But a fallen ruler her own subjects had come to abhor.

They called her a whore,
Who'd murder her husband and shamelessly take another.
Who lived not with honour,
But as a helpless sinner.

But no, she did not blame them.
For they were unknowing and afar,
When she was imprisoned at Castle Dunbar.
By Lord Bothwell and his men, strong and armed.
And within those impenetrable walls a queen was harmed.

Lord Bothwell forced himself on her,
And Mary lost something she had had forever.
She lost her courage and reluctantly married her bane,
An act that finally ended Mary's crumbling reign.

Another tear fell on her sweater
When a messenger arrived to her chamber.
She wiped her cheeks and hysterically unsealed the letter.
It wasn't from Elizabeth, but from her son.

Before reading the letter,
Mary embraced it, trying to feel it better.
A decade had passed since she last saw him,
Her handsome son James, now a crowned king.

Her eyes filled with desperate tears.
Was James sending a diplomat for her release?
Or perhaps an army to stir Elizabeth's heart with fear?
She couldn't believe her tragedy was coming to an end.

But when her joyous eyes saw her only son's words,
Within an instant, vanished her dreams, her hopes, and shaken was
her world.
James refused to arrange her escape,
And Mary stared at the letter, agape.

Cursed be such a devilish child.
Damned be his aspirations, his hopes, his dreams.
Let the evil fate run wild
And scorched shall be his realm.

But Mary did not ill-wish her son.
Though raised by her enemies, he was her son after all,
In this darkness, he had been her only sun.
And after this sunset, she made darkness her strength.

Nineteen years had gone,
And Mary found herself at the center of the Babington Plot.
She did not want to harm her cousin,
But desperate was the fallen Queen of Scots.

And Mary walked right towards Death's door,
For red-handed she was caught.
Treason was a crime the Queen of England couldn't ignore.
Thus, around Mary's neck tightened destiny's knot.

And fell the mighty Queen of Scots
For an act foreign to her heart
By family foreign
On soil foreign

All for reign.

A.K. HATA

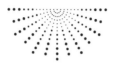

BIOGRAPHY

A.K. Hata loves to lose herself in fantastical worlds far away between the stars, filled with magic and wonder. She also writes and draws when she is not roaming through the park with her children. Her stories have been published in various anthologies and online publications. Visit her website.

OF ROBBERS AND DRAGONS

magic
sparkling wonders
in untamed lands
a quest awaits us
adventure

heroine
suspects nothing
watering the crops
what will happen next
expectations

raiders
attacking farms
kidnapping her brother
she has to act
suspension

hope
still alive
reunite her family

hasty preparations are made
departure

quest
desperate venture
looking for clues
will she find him
determination

dragon
diamond scales
circling the air
death looming above her
fear

surprise
a trap
in the forest
she is caught
will this end well
questions

spitefulness
despicable trait
raider are laughing
the heroine's quest failed
despair

finale
the dragon
devouring the robbers
saving the two children
happy-end

DARK WINTER

Winter's dead, capitalists sold her head.
Sour rain falls on barren lands,
your future lies in your own hands.

ROBBED

Her heart shatters in the sudden silence,
no echo of the outer world pervades.
Unutterably pain makes everything seem timeless,
her soul pierced with a billion blades.
Darkness dawns, as hope now fades.

On his face, such a peaceful countenance,
agleam by the dying sun's last light.
Missing movement gives doubt sustenance,
his beloved soul has taken flight.
Deserted his body, entering eternal night.

Without an anchor, forever lost her balance,
without his love, how shall she live?
Unbearable the silence of his absence,
darkness devours her, leaving only grief.
Unexpected hit the world's most cunning thief.

ANOTHER WEEK

house-tiger
lazying around
soft, silky fur
a perfect Sunday afternoon
regenerate

skyscrapers
standing tall
shiny, reflective symmetry
back to the office
busy

weekend
coming soon
forecast: cloudless sky
hope on the horizon
daydreaming

HAIKUS

An icy wind blows.
Cherry blossom petals fall,
like tears from my eyes.

Darkness covers me.
I'm always invisible,
outshined by the stars.

I am forgetting,
feeling safer every day—
till he's here again.

The magic abates,
the warmth of day is fading.
Will no one save me?

The words are flowing,
it's too late to stop them now.
They can't be unsaid.

A lonely wolf sits,

singing for his lost soulmate,
now roaming the sky.

Longing and searching,
we are always on the run,
missing out on life.

The dream is fading,
bleak reality returns.
My eyes stay empty.

My heart, torn apart,
red pain leaving my body,
soon I'll be gone too.

An endless blackness,
undefeated, unchallenged,
hiding all the stars.

My soul is crying,
inaudible to others,
I suffer alone.

I am torn apart.
Logic advices one thing,
my heart another.

Cold ice burns my skin,
my blood is crystallizing,
darkness closing in.

Colors fade away,
without you my life is black.
Please brighten my sky.

PATRICK WINTERS

BIOGRAPHY

Patrick Winters is a graduate of Illinois College in Jacksonville, IL, where he earned a Bachelor of Arts degree in English Literature and Creative Writing and achieved membership into Sigma Tau Delta, an international English honors society. Winters is now a proud member of the Horror Writers Association, and his work has been published in the likes of *Sanitarium Magazine*, *Deadman's Tome*, *Trysts of Fate*, and other such titles. A full list of his previous publications may be found at his author's site, if you are so inclined to know: http://wintersauthor.azurewebsites.net/Publications/List

BONES

I long to test boundaries and seek horizons;
To chase down the sun and terrify the night;
To carry the earth, lest it carry me away first;
To ascend to skies that have fast held me down;
To stare a star in the eye before leaving it behind;
To paint the firmament with my own colors --
In short, to wrest a still-wild soul
From this anchor of bones.

VONNIE WINSLOW CRIST

BIOGRAPHY

Vonnie Winslow Crist is author of *The Enchanted Dagger, Owl Light, The Greener Forest*, and other award-winning books. Her fiction is published in Amazing Stories, Cast of Wonders, *Killing It Softly 2, Dragon's Lure, Potter's Field 4 & 5, The Great Tome of Dragons and Draconic Lore, Best Indie Speculative Fiction: 2018*, and elsewhere. A cloverhand who has found so many four-leafed clovers that she keeps them in jars, Vonnie strives to celebrate the power of myth in her writing.

For more information, visit http://www.vonniewinslowcrist.com

MAGIC

Love is a magician's trick:
optical illusions, holograms,
false walls, sleight of hand...

Peek behind the silk curtain—
you'll find escape hatches,
flimsy bindings, hidden agendas,
and surprise endings.

Wait—nothing up the sleeve?
No special effects designed
to fool eyes and ears?
It looks like the real thing?

Then, grab hold—
for on this high-tech planet where
even our dreams are controlled
by machines manufacturing
a happier, more productive tomorrow,

there is little love, and less magic
left.

TRANSFORMED

A door closes,
and I stand on field-stone path
that meanders through violets and catnip.

The soles of my feet absorb thyme-scent
as I dash
from garden to thicket to dense forest.

I pause, stroke
spongy bark rippling around trees,
too ancient for ax.

Dimness presses on my eyes.
I slump, ear-to-soil, and hear
the muffled thump of hooves.

As I rise, turn to run,
the king and his huntsmen appear
at the top of the hill.

With images of white deer

and bloody wounds flashing through
my skull, I mournfully whisper,

"Can't you see—I'm not deer, but woman."
Laughing, my pursuers notch their arrows,
draw their bows, and shoot.

WOLF-BIT

An amber wink
and you quick-step into Granny's cottage.

Ignoring my mother's warning,
I loll in musky warmth
until you lunge, sink teeth,
tear open, slink away...

Wolf-bit,
I wrap my scarlet cloak tightly
around shoulders, and guided
by light from Mars's sibling moons,
tramp the dangerous paths
searching
for a triangle of familiar face
looming in the howl of midnight.

Ever hungry, never satisfied --
I wander the red-tinged landscape
hunting for you

in this fairy-tale
of evolution.

REMEMBERING

Auctioneer was coming the next day—
so I agreed to spend the day
emptying the attic for a great aunt
too feeble to climb a ladder
and haul down the trunks.

Almost lunchtime, I reached behind a chest,
gripped a dead man's mandolin.
It was shaped like a gourd, rough-skinned,
striped, with twelve wires
(three of which were broken).

Carried across the Atlantic centuries before,
its Old World beginnings
were as clear as a familiar melody.
I wondered, "In which castle were you played?
And who there listened to your song?"

Closing my eyes, I pictured:
stone walls draped with tapestries
of stag hunts and jousting matches,

women wrapped in fur-trimmed cloaks,
and dogs arguing over discarded bones.

With a will of their own, my fingertips
plucked a melancholy scattering of notes.
Overwhelmed, I pressed a damp cheek
to it's mottled belly—
remembering.

I have never played
a stringed instrument in this life,
yet my thumbs, fingers, palms, and temples
ached
with long ago songs of mandolin.

CHAGALL'S VILLAGE

My viridian face, angled and planed,
noses out the future.
My ghost lips repeat dead men's tales.
My spirit eye gazes through crystal,
glimpses puzzle pieces
which mesh to form a jigsawed heritage.

A Prussian blue cow, still wearing
the witch-woman's protection beads,
stares at me.
We both recall the auburn-haircd milkmaid
who smelled like new-mowed hay.

Above our heads, Vitebsk
folk-dances on the Russian snow,
shoots smoke into an inky background.

Bound for a cottage, my fieldworker father
nods to his wife's knees—
for my mother, once again, has turned
the village upside-down with her songs.

An Orthodox giant fills the church vestibule
as he ponders
the crucifix clutching my windpipe.

Look, O Holy Man,
I wear Grandfather's garnet ring on the hand
that lifts a sprig of dream-plant
to the center of my timepiece.

I have faith
that each flower petal, each grain of pollen,
each fruit fragment that falls from this branch
will spark a vision.

Then, I,
color-lover, surrealist, mystic
will paint a fantasy.

WRITING AT THE LIBRARY

Hardbacks, paperbacks, and pamphlets
stacked tall as my shoulder
lean against the wall.

Ready for the used-book sale,
the paper towers
hold millions of words.

I lift my pen, wonder,
will someone read the poems
and stories I've written?

Tomorrow, I will return,
purchase a bag of discarded books
and listen to the authors whispering.

For this place is a sanctuary,
the glow filtering down from its skylight
is as soft as dreams,

and the words trapped
on those yellowed pages murmur
my name.

DEBTS

The fattish grandmother
carries a purse of coffins.
With a snap, her pocketbook's flap
opens like an oven door
and a tattooed wrist vanishes in leather.

She withdraws a hankie
to dab at a reservoir of mass graves,
then hoists up sagging shoulders,
listens as names are proclaimed:
mother, papa, brothers, aunts, uncles...

Concentration camp survivors know
nations could build a hundred monuments,
letter a thousand plaques,
issue a million apologies,
and still

owe a debt.

LUNCH WITH A GODDESS

At a curry-scented restaurant,
three women share *pakoras*,
samosas, saag paneer,
basmati rice, *dal*, and *chapatis*
while melodies of flute and string
fill the room with song.
We smile,
chat about books, writing, and art.

I study the empty chair at our table,
the bubbling fountain nearby,
and on the wall, the map of a river.
Labeled the *Ghaggar-Hakra*,
it is shown winding through
Punjab, Haryana and Rajasthan.

I prefer its more poetic name:
Sarasvati.
For what river could be lovelier
than one named after a deity
of wisdom, music, and the arts.

I touch the swan brooch at my throat.
It is as pale
as rice flour patterns poured on floors,
as an Ocean of Milk,
as a poet's dream of sacred beauty.

I do not believe in coincidence.
On this sun-swept day
when magic seems to pour through the windows
with the daylight,
I sway, ever so slightly, to the music
and open my heart
to Saraswati's blessing.

JAYDE REIDER

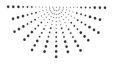

BIOGRAPHY

The product of two well-known authors, Jayde's goal is to step out of their spotlight and create his own. Dabbling primarily in science fiction and old-fashioned horror, his long awaited debut will be arriving soon.

In the meantime, he follows his wife around like a lost puppy as she professionally plays classical music. He hopes to settle down in Canada one day to be closer to family while enjoying the frozen north.

TELL ME

Tell me
How do you tell the one you don't love to go away?
That the very friendship once so grand has frayed.
It was not an ill-act that led everything to stray
But the realization that moving on is not possible while the world is
still grey.

Tell me
How do you tell the one who has never known love?
They cling and they whine when push comes to shove.
Books and movies have tainted their ideals of a beloved
And they will not see reason when steeped in puppy love.

Tell me
How do you tell the one who will never listen?
If they would but sit down, they could see what they're missing.
The dark days of sadness and longing, the drifting
Until then, they will never understand or be forgiving.

DESPAIR

Depression is a word many hear
Everyone thinks lightly on a topic so drear
Spending time looking down on us with a sneer
Partly wondering why we hold atrocities so dear
Apart from others using methods to wallow in, like beer
Intricate ways of escaping cross minds when no one lends an ear
Regrets do not frighten us, but yet we are here.

FADE

Some days I just want to fade away
The world keeps passing by in a haze
People always claim it is merely a faze
But life consistently feels more like a maze.

L.L. NELSON

BIOGRAPHY

L.L. Nelson is a full time librarian, part time genealogist, history buff, and word nerd with a passion for poetry and 'what ifs'. Favorite poems include Beowulf, The Odyssey, and The Raven, among many others. She lives in Southern California with her husband and children.

RAINSTORM

It's been a while since I've woken to a rainstorm –
That's the price of waking in 'paradise' every morn.
They say, *it usually doesn't rain in Southern California*
Contrast that to a humid childhood in the middle of Virginia

My days proceed, with children and work, until I am worn down.
That night, for the first time in ages, I sleep sound.
When I awake to rain in the morning,
I think I hear the sprinklers crowing.

But this morning,
On windows of my ubiquitous, dust darkened building,
I awoke to dimmed skies
And the pitter-patter from the heavens' eyes.

The *river* had come, and with it, rain –
Rain to heal, rain to chill, rain to let me breathe again.
For a minute, I stood, letting the rain, my chaos, drown,
With the furious raindrops, cleaning the city, the town

INTELLECTUALLY LAZY

Theory states that truth
is never absolute.
And to believe
is to err.
At least, that's what *he* said.

Yet no theory has satisfied me
like the one that states that
there is absolute truth.

Not one meal offered
at this potluck of ideas
has filled me, like
the soul food
of my childhood.

But to believe,
to take pleasure,
in the soul food
of ideas taught
at a tender age –

Is to be Lazy?

To be assured
of my beliefs.
To know that
my beliefs
sustain me –

Is to reject Intelligence?

I accept that
my beliefs are
not your own
I accept that
we view the world
differently.

But to tell me
that my beliefs
relegate me
to a lack of drive...

Speaks not to my work ethic –

But to your maturity.

PHOENIX WITHIN

Fire

I learned to fear the fire
That which crackled and simmered beneath my skin
It was too dangerous, in need of extinguishing.
And yet, I knew it protected me.

Pain

There is a pain, far worse than physical ailments,
Of rejection, of no longer existing
Where you once belonged.
But one cannot ignore the heat
That embers give
When touched so carelessly.

Rebirth

Channel your power, but do not be overwhelmed
You are in the fire, under the fire
Grace under fire as you are reborn

Reborn into what you will one day become
Do not fear the pain.
It will purify you.
It will heal you.
And in turn, you will heal others.
Be a predator of evil
Not to be trifled with.

BALLAD OF BJORNULF - PART 1

O Lusarth! Hail to me, Hallmund thy humble voice,
As I invoke the illustrious image of
Bjornulf the Bold, Bjornulf the Beloved, Bjornulf
The Tamer of thunder and Tenelth's *haldraga*!
O Lusarth! Help me, thy *haldraga* Hallmund speak
Of the alliance, Bjornulf authored and aligned
'Twixt daring men and an ancient dragon's descent,
That Lohikarran warriors and legends leap
To honor oaths made by our originator.

Lo! In a land so long forgotten, was once forged
An aethling foretold to ascend against his kin.
Borne Bjornulf, a babe sent out to bury at sea.
Death demured the gift. That - was detained by dragons.
Bjornulf bore the name of dragon bred, as he bled
Fighting fearsome mainland foes of his Tenelth.
The winged warriors of wretched doom, they wail!
His people, persecuted by the perilous.
But Bjornulf born barbarous and dragon bred, slew
Many the terrible teemings with Tenelth. That
Kin of his - carried cacophony for days. Lo!

Ancient dragon feuds over frosted firmament
Drew Tenelth to disturb the devil, Ryluth.
Wisdom wielded by the warrior, Bjornulf won
The fair land of Lohikarra from the loathsome
Powers at last. Pushed back from peril, the people
Of Lohikarra lauded Bjornulf as their lord.

Fairest lady of Lohikarra, Freya fought
The dragons with dire determination, once a
Sacrifice for respite from sinister serpents.
Her calling since childhood, now censured by Bjornulf.
She, daughter of Drifor, chief of the Droquro
And Ruddea, regal priestess to Ryluth,
Brought her bed-roll before Bjornulf, cloak-bare and bade
Him husband, heretofore pledged herself to grim death.
In short season, she bore him babes of his body,
Numbering the thegn names of Lohikarra now.
Thus the twelve thegns' descent in all, from thence time called
Freya, fairest mother; fond was Bjornulf's consort.

Waxing in war-fame, the Droquro went willing,
Following their fearsome leader, Bjornulf to the
Mighty mead hall and mound of Tenelth's making.
The dignity of Drattujërt drove many to Bjornulf's banner.
Still Ryluth rose and reigned in terror, Tenelth
Never sleeping, never silent, soaring over
Drattujërt, until the destined demise of vile
Ryluth - To languish and lament in Lyrroth e'er.

Ryluth! The revulsion with which you're regarded,
Only pales to your pernicious powers. Once a
Terrible team with Tenelth, the treachery
Of your gilded lust of gold and power, gained you foes.
As Bjornulf brandished the battle-sword and slew more
Of your terrible kin, Tenelth took to the
Sky, scouring the grassy sea of Svarhestån,

To deal you thy destined demise. Yet darkness fell
As Tenelth traded his life for your triumph.
You sinister serpent, slipping away, sulking
As Bjornulf, broken, begged his dragon brother live.
Yet Tenelth soon slept a dying slumber, save
To console Bjornulf's childish heart. He spoke once
Of lifelong bond and band between Bjornulf and him.
And thus Tenelth titled Bjornulf *haldraga*.
Alight in spirit, Bjornulf's alarmed spirit stilled -
Joined in joyous match, Bjornulf and Tenelth were
One body, two souls, which wavered not in power
But Bjornulf born, at Tenelth's death, a boundless
And mighty man, first master of *Haldraganem*.

Oh, Lusarth! Derive to me dragon dreams, so I
May speak the majesty of Bjornulf's memories.
When once he witnessed the wonder *Haldraganem*.
And spoke as sublime serpents do, soaring over
Lohikarra, in its lavish grandeur. Bjornulf
Here, heard the harkening tribes plead help from Ryluth's
Devilish dragon kin and Tenelth's decree
That the tribes unite in tribute to their brave king.
Bjornulf, dragon bred, divined his due destiny
And Tenelth assured his achievement of such
Would Bjornulf, his wanderers and descent worship
Tenelth and his kin, from thence time to the end.
A vow Bjornulf made, to his virtue and victory.
When winter's light woke Bjornulf, he wept but little
Baring Tenelth's bones to brave Drattujërt's bury-
Mound. The mead hall made with melancholy music
Lamenting those, alas, lately lain in Mirroth.
Aft three days mourning the dead, Bjornulf departed
To wrench wretched Ryluth from his deep mountain roost
And disavow the land of b'deviled dragons.

XIMENA ESCOBAR

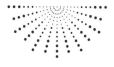

BIOGRAPHY

Ximena is an emerging author of short stories and poetry. Originally from Chile, she is author of a translation into Spanish of the Broadway Musical *The Wizard of Oz* (2012), and of an original adaptation of the same, *Navidad en Oz* (Christmas 2018).

Clarendon House Published her first piece in the UK with *The Persistence of Memory* (*Fireburst* a Flash Fiction Anthology 2018), and Literally Stores her first online publication with *The Green Light*. She has also had several micro pieces accepted into Black Hare Press and Blood Song Books Anthologies, which will be published later this year.

Organic Ink is releasing her first attempts at poetry!

She lives in Nottingham with her husband and three children.

THE SELFIE

They were the glow of wonder, lingering like beauty. More beautiful because it's lost.

Games of hide and seek in the maze. The back of her dress disappearing in the darkest shades of green; in the darkest dark where they loved each other most.

They were children in a hideaway; dear dark wardrobe in the beginning of memory. Like a forest in the depth of their soul – siblings hugging knees, side by side, absorbed in the distant sight of stars, open sky between the high branches.

Had it been 12 years since they last saw each other?

They sat on the fountain – his arm wasn't long enough to see the dry statues behind them, nor the balcony above with the curtain billowing; but their view was deep as infinite, and they travelled all the way to that day that became every day, right there on that stone (the only time she did smell of mandarins).

And they smiled their underwhelming smile – they weren't as attractive as they used to be. But both inbreathed the cosmic story overfilling their lungs, and emotion lit their eyes within the frame of the phone (glossy and expensive, like his Rolex, like they always knew the future should look but neither believed they would ever accomplish).

They were misfits, really; a couple of losers in a costume of Italian lovers, as funny fountain drizzle exploded on their faces like wonderful ideas; cheeks rising, dimples sinking.

The hole in the gut sinking. The gap between the trees opening.

And waves of red hair cascading down her shoulders like a winding path to the dark corners of desire.

They turned a corner in the maze, months later. They got lost in his mother's bedroom. His tongue circled inside her, like a spiral chasing the centre; the elusive definition of their love. It was his first and last time with a woman.

But they found the tree in the middle; its everlasting fruits of everlasting rum; everlasting swelling of throats and verses, featuring oranges and Italian palaces.

They were so drunk in love, but so out of love too; because it's flesh that stands the reality of a shared life. They cried deliciously in each other's arms, letting the divergence ahead overflow.

Little palms unsticking in the starry sky.

Having to go through it all, alone.

The Rolex said it was 6pm. This time tomorrow they'll be hugging each other goodbye on the platform; possibly for the last time as they each return to their respective hemispheres – She to the children, He to his lover. Neither wanted a hangover and both were disappointed that those days were truly over. Yet, they swirled their Aperol Spritzers and it seemed a blink before they found themselves swimming, fully clothed, in the forbidden sunrise. Taking selfies of a delightful shine.

The ineradicable memory of their love.

THE AFFAIR

Her certainty
A bond, inscribed
"He loved us more than he loved himself".
His tombstone
Gravity
(Seat at the table
Invitations)

Some envelopes smell of gardenias
Carnivorous
Relentless
Weight on her soul

A bond, strengthened
Like stones (in pockets)
Slithering serpent
Streams cold
Choking her.

He is no longer but betrayal
In her tombstone.

AN OCEAN OF GIN AND TONIC

I can hear you talking
Through the water

Pirate eye tunnel
Is my reflection

My skull
My fish tale,
My fairy tale,

Don't look down on me
Pull me
Kiss my red wine lips
Fuck my fears away

SPRING

Girl sprouting
In the flutter of eyelids
Like Blossom
Imperceptible
Wind of butterflies
Under the covers
Under the t-shirt
Girl disappearing
In woman
Dreams unaccomplished
In flame
Reduced to ashes
Green grass
Under baby's soles

SWEET LITTLE CHILDREN

In a sweet English village
covered in snow
lived a sweet little girl
with a strawberry bow
and a sweet little boy
with a chocolate sledge
caramel boots
Footprints
on the edge
of a garden

Like he could escape.

The sweetness
in those giant honeycomb eyes
That peculiar spark
of sugar and mischief
like sweet little children
sitting in crescent moons
magic

steaming the bedroom mirror
as she licks sweet lips
and rubs her tummy.
Can't wait for Christmas morning.

DOLL PARTS

"I won't talk about the past anymore", she said. "I'm only talking about what will happen from now on." "I'm using this pain to make something wonderful".

He held her hand, like he had so many times. Her masculine hands. Creative hands for making wonderful things. Like her saddest smile.

But pain stung her like acid, welling up and blurring the bus window, the hideous yellow foam peeping through the torn seat cover. She looked up at the dangling handles, defying her tears (it helped imagining a leather and yellow foam dress.)

The handles swayed with the bus stopping. She clasped the seat in front – composed, just then, by the physicality of inertia. By the loud door opening. By the loud woman who obviously knows the driver and wants everybody to know it, laughing her way off. Look at her, still waving from the pavement. Look at the hideous day. It's not even grey. It's brown.

"He doesn't see me…. It's bad enough that he won't look at me; but he doesn't even perceive me in the periphery… It's sad, because I can still love that about him, you know? Because he's decided; and I always admired how he can decide so bluntly; separate the wheat from the chaff…"

He looked at her beautiful hand; her masculine hand circling the air when she talked. That's the Italian in her. And her doll-like features. Skin darker than skin. Eyes greener than green eyes. Her natural hair color looks fake too.

"… But this is just… Honest, plain, brutal… Indifference..."

A space opened in her lungs, cold and huge like her front door opening, and his things not being there. A void that opened under her feet. Like when he said, 'I don't love you anymore'.

"He's not trying to protect his decision… He's not trying not to feel… This is just absolute, brutal, absence of feeling... Not even his sweater touched me, when I leaned over for the jug… Even when I was exuding my energy like a stink, he was oblivious… God... I pulled so much... I pulled and kept pulling the finest, most invisible thread of fluff left between us -I said to Sarah loud so he could hear it 'the cucumbers made the sandwiches soggy', little things that should remind him of us, little winks, you know-, but he's made of ice... He didn't pick up the extra cup I filled with water. He filled himself another one."

Bryan's hand on her hand squeezed gently. And she saw the Off-Licence just then, through the glass, and felt home, for a second, before pressing the buzzer like a cliff-hanger. Like her feet were dangling in infinity.

Press the loud buzzer again. How many heads do I see? Things I can count. Things I can touch. Two steps down. My yellow Doc Martens on the pavement.

"I'll be ok. I'll stop talking about it, when we get home."

"I know" Said Bryan. He smiled the saddest smile, but she only saw the man walking his dog.

There was the building. She imagined her body plummeting from the balcony. Arms and legs twisted right there, like her mannequins. That would make a beautiful sculpture.

Her heart beat loudly, slowly. Not in a distracting way – this was happening inside her, like the scary music in a movie enhancing fear as the key inserts into the keyhole. In real life, she was looking for the keys in her pocket. Bryan was looking at her young blue vein; all the pain running through her beautiful young hand. Hands that made beautiful things. Fantastic things.

She clasped the doorframe. Archie won't bark – that's one thing she won't miss on her fabrics, his fur everywhere. But his computers will be gone; his music. The closet. The empty closet. The emptiness will be there. The emptiness in her chest.

He took his mum's carpet too. The walls looked wider; greyer; in the shade of that hideous brown-grey day.

"I'm putting all my things in here. My sewing machine, everything."

She imagined her colorful paraphernalia piled up against the walls, but she felt sick underneath it all. Deep down, buried under every other truth, she wanted to do something wonderful *for him*. So that he heard of it. So that he admired her, wished he'd never left her.

She gripped the toilet seat. Veins ran swollen, up her arms – her silent scream, begging him to notice her, to remember, gushing out of her mouth like a torrent of doll parts; her fragmented soul. She will find the remnant of his love somewhere in his subconsciousness. She will rest her head in the sweet pillow of that certainty, because he has cut all ties, to the last thread, but true love doesn't die, and her art did speak to him once.

Or maybe love was just fluff brushing fluff. Maybe love was just fingerprints kissing on plastic cups, at work.

She looked in the mirror – Bryan was standing behind her. Her heart leaped – she hadn't seen him since he died; since he stormed off from the solicitor's, two weeks before his accident.

Matt hated her talking to Bryan. It was just too much for him, crossing the line between quirkiness and madness. If he could only see Bryan now, gaining matter and particles and flesh as she breathed. Each. Overwhelmed. Breath.

"It's time I went, babe".

Her hand rose silently to cover her mouth, like a scared doll. A bellow that didn't materialize and was sucked, instead, by the immensity of a dreadful door opening. Bryan had opened the bedroom door too; found her legs, her beautiful plastic legs intertwined with Matt's but, despite her unimaginable regret, she never stopped feeling complete. She loved Matt so. And the accident wasn't her fault; motorbikes were always dangerous.

"I'm so sorry" she said – looking into his eyes, on the glass.

"I know."

The electrifying nearness of his body intensified. She longed to turn around and hug him, cry on the pillow of his chest. But what if he wasn't there anymore when she did.

She wanted goodbye to last forever.

AGUALUNA IN THE BALCONY

She lifts little heels
Creasing
Patent leather shoes
That daddy gave her

If she could climb down,
Twirl herself around
plaits
Like a jelly snake

But she wants to be the rabbit
in the Hole of daddy's hugs
Squeezing her lungs
Constricting her

If air could be clear water rising
like when tears well up
I'd skydive through the waves.

I swim underwater
I hear the whale singing

Swaying
Like when daddy carried me
Gentle teeth pulling me
down
By the frill of my sock

She wants to play
But my heart beats like men marching
And the whale worries.

She shoots up to save me,
so fast that when she breaks through the surface,
I project through my own mouth
I skyrocket out of my own mouth like a shooting star
And I never look down

When the dandelion puff blows
Against the asphalt

C.A. MACKENZIE

BIOGRAPHY

Cathy writes poems, short stories, and essays, some of which appear online and in various print anthologies and other publications. She has self-published several books of poetry and compilations of short stories. Her first novel, Wolves Don't Knock, a psychological drama, was published in July 2018. Visit her website.

SNAKE EYES

My insides coil and recoil
like a serpent spiralling
through my spine
and I cringe at the pain
—and you

Your snaky eyes
glow in the dark
before your mouth opens wide
to spew venom
onto my face

I wipe it off,
calmly,
while you watch
behind your veneer
of viciousness

Acidity boils
through my veins,
yet I rein it in,

not letting it out

A heavy weight crashes on me,
overpowering me
as I intertwine about you
and collapse within myself

And I see a thousand stars
shining in the sky.

STACEY JAINE MCINTOSH

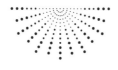

BIOGRAPHY

Stacey Jaine McIntosh was born in Perth, Western Australia where she still resides with her husband and their four children.

Although her first love has always been writing, she once toyed with being a Cartographer and subsequently holds a Diploma in Spatial Information Services.

Since 2011 she has had over two dozen short stories and drabbles printed for online consumption and in various anthologies, both in print and forth coming. She has also had two poems accepted for publication.

Stacey is also the author of Solstice, Morrighan & Lost and she is currently working on several other projects simultaneously.

She specialises in writing Paranormal Romance and Celtic inspired fairy tales.

When not with her family or writing she enjoys reading, photography, genealogy, history, Arthurian myths and witchcraft.

Discover more at www.staceyjainemcintosh.com

PETALS

Blood red liquid,
Spilled across the floor.
Deathsweet petals and human hair,
All things that curses take.
A witch cackles,
while the cauldron bubbles.

DARKNESS

When the night is dark,
And the moon is full.
Wolves howl,
Trees whisper.
She rides the wind,
Like a moth.
On paper wings,
She flutters.
Falling,
As hearts collide.

CINDY O'QUINN

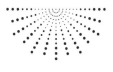

BIOGRAPHY

Cindy O'Quinn is an Appalachian writer who grew up in the mountains of West Virginia.

In 2016, Cindy, along with her husband and sons, made the move from Virginia to the northern woods of Maine and started homesteading.

She has had a longtime love of everything horror, thanks to her mom who started her at a very young age. They spent many a weekend in the 70's going to the local drive in theaters.

Cindy is the author of *Dark Cloud on Naked Creek*, and the dark poetry collection, *Return to Graveyard Dust*, which made it to the 2017 HWA Bram Stoker preliminary ballot.

Her work has been published or is forthcoming in *Twisted Book of Shadows*, the *HWA Poetry Showcase Vol. V, Nothing's Sacred Vol. 4 & 5, Rag Queen Periodical, Moonchild Magazine, Sanitarium Magazine,* and others.

Member of HWA, NESW, NEHW, SFPA, Horror Writers of Maine, and Weird Poets Society.

You can follow Cindy for updates on Facebook @CindyOQuinnWriter, Instagram cindy.oquinn, and Twitter @COQuinnWrites.

TOUCHED BY MADNESS

Sanity can be purchased, temporarily, with a prescription—not yet available over-the-counter.

I saw six nuns the day I met insanity, or maybe they were ravens. It's hard to say with any amount of certainty, with all that black swishing about. Obsidian feathers or fabric, take your pick. It floated towards me or away. Ominous was the feeling that touched me most.

Awake—unable to move as darkness returned from behind a full moon, and into the corners, made of shadows that visited me in my room.

Even lunacy sounded logical when the screams were timed just so. Songs of madness rang against unwitting ears as they called for someone to know—the answer, that is. Path of life, stained red with blood. Or tears. Or both.

Morning came, and the sun rose as I shook away the cobwebs from the long night. Spoke your mantra before my feet could ever hit the floor.

Dark is not a color…it's a place where I spent most days, waiting to leave or simply be erased. Touched by madness and the darkness it creates. I'm left alone with six ravens, or maybe they're nuns, neither of which could be considered much fun.

In the company of darkness for too many years to consider, while I hid myself away from the world. When I realized it came from within, I was free to leave that darkness again.

I failed to keep the crazy outside—no matter what I did or how hard I tried. To hide, that is.

DARKEST ECHO

The sound of your voice – inside my head
when I woke from yesterday's song,
reminders of how it felt to be dead.

Facing darkness – when it's left unfed.
Tears from the sun, cloud against pain, and
the sound of your voice – inside my head.

Regretting the words – left unsaid,
my days remaining will not be long,
reminders of how it felt to bc dead.

All the words written – never to be read,
lost forever without a name.
The sound of your voice – inside my head.

Unable to move – legs heavy like lead,
try to be included – wanting to belong,
reminders of how it felt to be dead.

The color of death – the feeling of dread,
I tried to leave you, but knew it was wrong.
The sound of your voice – inside my head,
reminders of how it felt to be dead.

FRACTURE

The fractured voices carry from my mind,
onto paper or computer screen.
All fighting for the front of the line,
so many characters wanting to scream.

I let them out – one at a time.
The need for more room,
all that I can find.
Don't pretend to know – don't try to assume.

I'll have my quiet,
when they have all had a turn.
Their lives written on paper,
all hard lessons to learn.

Thousands of yellowed pages
hiding without reason,
waiting like wine as it ages
to be released into an unnamed season.

Fractured voices
coming from fractured minds,
belonging to fractured souls,
that I long ago left behind.

THE ULTIMATE BAKER

Tears from my mouth
Bled into my soul
And reminded me of forever.

I ate your shadow
And made flour
From your bones.

Salted with pain
I baked a hefty loaf
Ate until you were no more.

Seeking out tomorrow
Proved a useless chore
Of my wasted hours.

I carefully chose
Which memories to keep
And let all others--
B-U-R-N

WATCHING

I watch
do you watch?
Like slipping in a dvd,
and kicking back.
That's how we watch
people walk by.
Why not order in,
and split the cost?
The show goes on all night
free of charge.
We can play a game,
and guess the lovers,
or who's on a first date,
and there won't be a second.
Wouldn't it be crazy
if we were being watched?
You just never know
who might be watching.
I did have the strangest feeling
walking through my kitchen,

in only my robe.
Thought it best to stop,
and strike a pose
just in case the microwave converted,
and was snapping a photo.

CATCHING

When insanity runs in the family,
it's not unusual to question your own –
Sanity, that is.
Someone once asked,
"Can you catch it?"
Like it's floating through the air
on the wings of a fucking sneeze.

My answer is always the same,
"Hell no, it's not catching."
But in that dark area of my mind,
the shadowy place,
that I keep hidden
from the sane world.
I continue to watch for the traces.

Often looking in the mirror,
just a glance to make sure
it's still me looking back,
and not those hollow eyes

that took my relatives
for a ride on the crazy train.
No return tickets or explanations why.

Just a place to wait while it catches hold of me.

ANOTHER SATURDAY AFTERNOON

Wait for me, wait for me!
Bare feet – outgrown shoes.
Can I have a soda pop – pretty please.
Riding in pick-up trucks.
Spending time with you.
Another day at the stock sale,
It's Saturday afternoon.

Parked on a hillside,
Slamming my thumb.
Damn! That really hurts!
Feeding pigs,
And stepping in shit.
One more day – being with you.
Just another Saturday afternoon.

One side warm,
The other – way too frigging cold.
Black snake sunning
Against a rock wall.
Mind starts to open,

And memories unfold.
Saturday afternoon – early Fall.

I hear your voice
Carried on the wind.
Where two rivers meet
To create a gentle bend.
I see through you.
You're just a ghost.
Saturdays… I miss you most.

THOMAS STURGEON JR.

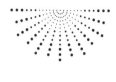

BIOGRAPHY

Thomas Sturgeon Jr is an author who is 33 years old. He first began writing at 13 years old. He loves to read and spend time with his family and friends despite his disabilities. He currently lives in Chatsworth, Georgia and currently wants more out of life. He's been published before with his poetry and currently has two short horror stories published in Weird mask magazine and in Deadman's Tome for the February 2019 issue. The short stories published were "The Dead City" and "Disturbed Valentine". Even though he struggles with thing's. He is currently at work on a horror short story collection and is loved by his family and friends. Despite being told by his teachers that he would never be published. He proved them wrong. He enjoys reading Stephen King among other horror authors and loves playing video games. Hoping to accomplish a feat in 2019 by getting his book published.

THE INJUSTICE

Hurt from the wrongful words you spoke
Even while I tried to get along with you

Inaccurate, not a word I said to you was negative
Nothing I say will make you believe me
Judgement I felt and I didn't deserve
Usefulness I was to you but you turned away
Seeing tomorrow as a new day of opportunities
Truth be told I'm relieved from you
In reality, I moved on not looking back
Cooling down from this depressive state
Even I will never again be your friend

TRAGIC LOVE

Reaching out to you, lost you so soon
Angels watching over me as I sleep
God knows that I tried to show you my love
Informed of your death months after you passed away
Coming from an age, your addiction to meth

Losing your battle to addiction
On some nights I remember your face
Verging on the path you took
Even though you made your choices I still miss you

LIFE ISN'T FAIR

In every choice I made the consequences deter
Facing obstacles in every form or another
Even though life dealt me the wrong deck of cards

In today I focus solely upon
Some days I just try to get through this hell
Nights alone, I face my trials with error
Tough I had to be when people trampled upon my kindness

Facing life each day, some days are good and bad
After 33 years of life
I still remain optimistic even though my days may seem dark
Remembering that this doesn't have to be what my future life is like

THE DARKEST LIE

Hurting from the distance from in between
Even though let people think whatever they may think

Darkest Lie, is to lie about the devil's existence
All the world experience times of death and hate
Recognizing that there's the cold hard truth
Keeping a roof over your head from the storms
Even when I avoid the negativity in my life
Sometimes life gets harder as it goes
Too see what others can't truly see for themselves

Lies people have told since the beginning of time
In even today as people live their lives
Even we all have sinned despite listening to the Darkest Lie

FINAL GOODBYES

In every death, there is a reminder of life once remembered
Now as I stand at the coffin with tears in my eyes
Always loved even when filled with regret
Listening to the sobs as a contact reminder of men's first sin

Grief is here, a heart having to heal over time
Over time, funerals have become too numerous to count
Often remembering their embrace when they were alive
Death comes to all, as heartbreaking that may seem
Becoming a survivor, telling others of recent times
Yet as we all must go on this walk of life
Even I know that there is a Heaven
So now I must say my final Goodbyes and live life again

STRUCTURE OF MIND

To think outside of common thinking
Reasoning I must have, to enjoy life
Urgent to write more
Cooling myself off during the summer heat
Truly recognizing that I mean so much to others
Using my skills from my creativity
Remembering the hardships as I move along
Counting down all my achievements
Determination is key to being known

Mostly I have to stay true to being original
I hope to build a career from writing
Now in a distant future as I walk along the beach
During life's more difficult trials
I pass this trial that's set before me

MARIA WILLIAMS

BIOGRAPHY

Maria Williams is a Queensland, Australia based poet. She has been writing poetry for her own enjoyment for the last fifty-seven years of her life but has looked to pursue professional publication only recently.

Her first poem titled *'Guns in the Distance'* was published in 2017 in the *Short and Twisted 2017* anthology by Celapene Press— a landmark event! Her recent poems *'On a Shelf in a Box'* and *'Boy on a Balcony'* will be published this year (2019) with Dragon Soul Press.

Maria likes to draw from the world around her to find inspiration for her work.

BOY ON THE BALCONY

The boy on the balcony,
Is looking outside.
He holds the rails tightly,
What is on his mind?

A cooler bag is on the floor,
Few flowers on the side.
There are no toys in the room,
What is on his mind?

Up high from the balcony,
He sees the world out there.
His tiny heart is filling up,
With pain and despair.

The rails on the balcony,
Protect him that's for sure.
But mum and dad were fighting,
For that he has no cure.

The boy on the balcony,

Is down on his knees.
Maybe he is trying painfully,
To understand all this.

His parents now live apart,
No love there anymore.
Maybe he is crying silently,
He is only...four.

ON A SHELF IN A BOX

She's done him wrong,
She's done him wrong.
The monster within,
Was far too strong.

The care she gave,
Was driven by love.
Believed she could manage,
With help from above.

Three angels descended,
She said, "This is it.
The monster together,
We now shall defeat."

The work now started,
She did what she did.
To rid the ugly face,
Of depression in him.

Put her needs and wants,

On a shelf in a box.
Left them for years,
Under key, under locks.

She wrapped him in wool,
To protect him from fall.
And fought all his fears,
And problems in all.

Feeling empty and alone,
Tells her man, she's not well.
He responds with Devil's voice,
"You have made my life hell."

After all she had done,
She is wondering why.
That the monster of depression,
Still is growing inside.

Now herself, needs some help,
Being old and so frail…
Turns her eyes on that shelf!!!
But the box…is not there.

Reaches up on the shelf,
With twisted, crooked hand.
To find her wants and needs,
Had turned by now into sand.

So, she sought some help,
From the ones that know.
Only to find out that,
She has done him wrong.

She is down, she is down,
She's hit a brick wall.

With nothing more to give,
She is an empty soul.

She had made room,
For his depression to grow.
By doing everything and now,
She had to change the show.

M. BRANDON ROBBINS

BIOGRAPHY

M. Brandon Robbins holds a Bachelor of English from Mount Olive College (now the University of Mount Olive) and a Master of Library Science from East Carolina University. He is currently employed full-time as a school librarian. His work has appeared in Shotgun Horror Clips and Trembling With Fear, and he is currently editing a novel for hopeful publication. Brandon blogs at www.mbrandonrobbins.com and was the writer of Library Journal's "Games, Gamers, and Gaming" column from 2012-2017. He lives in Goldsboro, NC with his wife and their ten pets and enjoys comic books and video games.

A VISIT FROM THE GRIM REAPER

Quiet breath of winter wind
Cloak—flick and flutter
Shadow passing
Shadow gone
Arrives alone
Alone, he is not, when he departs
Cloak—flick and flutter
Silence
Sleep for the living
When morning comes
The dead discovered.
Envied—they no longer fear
Quiet breath of winter wind
Cloak—flick and flutter

MY VAMPIRE

Drink of me
Long
Slow
Deep

My veins—
Collapsing

Skin as
Shriveled as
Dying
apples.

Drink of me
But I beg you
Not
To drink your fill.

For I must
Feed you

Once more
Twice more
Forever
more.

VANESSA BANE

BIOGRAPHY

Vanessa Bane dabbles in the art of romance alongside her well-known coauthor, J.E. Feldman. Vanessa's writing den changes location often as she travels the world with her husband and son. Inspiration for her characters and settings can be found scattered throughout the world, but particularly from Europe. Her aging soul will always answer to the beckoning call of the rolling hills of Ireland.

MY GUARDIAN

I know you're always there for me
But I don't always know how
Every time that I'm in trouble
You always seem to be around

EXTRAORDINARY

One day can be ordinary
The next could take you beyond your wildest dreams
Wherever it takes you, never be afraid
'Cause you're safe in the hands of fate

Anything is possible if you just believe
Everything could happen that you've never dreamed
Just take things day by day
'Cause the next day will be extraordinary

Just because one day goes wrong
It doesn't mean all your days are gone
Pick yourself back up and hold yourself tall
Tomorrow is a new day and it's extraordinary

DEPRESSION

Every time I hear your name
I cringe
Every time I hear a sad story
I cry

Now I watch
The sun float across the sky
How I wish I could know someone
Bright like it

Come on, find me
Do not worry about how
I won't stop screaming for help
'Til you show up on my doorstep

I would give anything to have
Someone to cheer me up
But no matter how much I scream
No one will ever come

PERSEVERANCE

Regardless of what stands in your way
    In your heart you know you can make it through
    Just don't give up and keep hanging on
    'Cause that's all you can do

BETRAYED

I've always been there as a friend
And maybe even more than that
But now I need your help

Don't turn away from me
You are my hope for happiness
More than ever before I need a hand

I thought I'd never see the day
When they would just turn away
Leaving me standing in the dust

Everything is falling apart
A broken heart still trying to beat
Being strangled by the dark

FOREVER SAD

I wish crying would make you forget
All the hurt you have ever felt

To cry away all the pain
To cry away all the hate
To cry away the helplessness
To cry away everything

Crying may release your weaknesses
But only for a moment

LET IT GO

The sea of unshed tears
Will most definitely overflow
Over time, one can only guess
What hurt you most
Don't hold it in - let it go

AMY LEDFORD

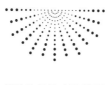

BIOGRAPHY

Born in North Carolina she always enjoyed reading and writing finding adventure in new stories until she was able to venture out and create her own. Settling down in Florida to raise her family she pursued a passion for poetry and now has multiple pieces published with many more to come.

As the words course through her veins and her heart breathes life into ink it leaves little room for doubt with readers of her abilities as a poetess. While they can feel the fires burning within her that force the pen to paper spilling the rawness of her soul out into verse.

SONNET III

I redefine people using my own light
Failing to uptake who they really are
Glossing reality over true sight
And misdirecting every hope thus far
Tipping the scales on the value they bear
Counter balanced by the weight of my flaws
Giving them undue credits that aren't there
Undermines my own worth without just cause
As the attributes given were not earned
They are who they are in masked disgrace
Then I'm left wondering how I got burned
Then I'm left wondering how I got burned
When I gave them the match in the first place
I've gotta learn to stop this toxic trait
That shields them in beauty I generate

SONNET IV

Shackled in the dungeons of memory
Ensnared by this subconscious tomb of pain
Dimming the light of the path before me
To wallow in unrepentant disdain
Slunk into such a sullen stricken stride
The quick sands of the hourglass do fall
Encapsulates the heartache wrought inside
To a dour hour of demise upon all
Hope abates to bask in loves brevity
As it lingers no longer than mere breath
That you suffocate in depravity
Then discard and leave to die its dire death

      What bliss it would be to one day break free
      These tormenting bonds imprisoning thee

NOT THE ONE FOR ME

Who is he, that he was able to generate such heartache?
That you're left bleeding words from your damaged soul
Using your shredded spirit of light as a weakened beacon among the
rough seas
To find a way past the tattered remnants he callously cast away
Who is he, that he was able to make you feel unworthy of love?
When your essence so clearly whispers promises of forever
And every drop of blood from the wounds his betrayal caused
Leave a lingering scent of loyalty
Misplaced though it was
Who is he, that you felt he deserved any of the beauty you have
within you?
Why would you want to give so much to someone who values so
little?
He used your hope to blind you
And his deceits stripped the core of your dignity raw
Who is he, that he didn't grab on and protect such a rare gem from
pain?
While you sacrificed the concept of trust based on the delusions he
fed your heart
Spoonfuls of sugar rationed out to garner your surrender

So his selfish ego could drain every ounce of your faithful devotion
Who is he, that he could so shamelessly lay false claims of possession?
Without upholding any honor of his own
It's too bad that the clarity of hind sight isn't available until the end
Once you've already been torn to pieces and left to come back from the dead
Alone and bruised and suffering with only the strength of your integrity left to lead
So who is he you ask while searching through my past
Not the one for me I say but a lesson that left a scar.

YOU MUST RISE

The presence of light doesn't change the nature of darkness.
Its purpose arises repeatedly as the shine fades away.
Casting its shadows like tentacles
Spreading out and entangling anything within reach.
Engulfing them into the bleak unseen
Its entry is tangible
As it creeps along distracting visibility with the illusion of depth.
Yet it offers only absence in its wake.
There's a sense of yearning that accompanies the night
A feeling so dire it snares your soul
Perhaps it's the devil whispering treacherous lies in his effort to
claim you
There is a beckoning solitude of silence in the expanse
Along with a false comradery among the like
Who are all suffering the turmoil of their own volition
By tucking grief, despair, anger, and loneliness around them
As a blanket to ward off the chill
But the host allows no warmth
For the pits of hell are cold and dank.
The darkness craves acceptance
Extending a vast array of deep crevices to conceal away your sins

That could be its allure on the surface
Out of sight out of mind
Yet really, it's a tomb sealing all that anguish in alongside you
Until you beseech the light to fall upon the tendrils of torment
And scatter the shadows back into their holes
Give yourself permission to bask in glory
Instead of snuffing out your spirit.
You must rise.

SOUL RITES

No matter how wide I open my eyes
to let the light in
there's no escaping the pull of eternal darkness
It's always present
even in times of utter joy
laying just beneath the surface ready to pounce
My whole world is a game of tug of war
hinging upon which side I feed
giving strength to fuel the upcoming victor
One misstep and my soul could be consumed
by foul forces hellbent on overpowering glory
ounce by glorious ounce
Detriment arises when the midnight sun is fullest
peaking between clouds
and strumming with a steady hum of menace
Driven by misdeeds and mistrust
to pave the sludgy path away from hope
while sinful wagers multiply amounts
The fates may weave the tale as it unfolds
but I'm the creator of my destiny
sifting through the choices hampered with disillusion

My spirit is the light
filtering past shadowy intents barricaded within turmoil
due to silent suffering I must renounce
Disheartened pain and panic thrive
as long as my karmic breath remains unclaimed
with a mangled cycle of diminished faith
But hell doesn't hold the sole rights
to the fire that burns inside me
give witness to the unextinguished flame as my will surmounts

I WANNA

I wanna bleed light across dimensions
Be inspired to transcend bounds
Feel exhilarated without limitations
And thrive with every experience
I wanna glow from the inside out
Offer hope to those in darkness
Lift them up past their pain
And conquer every fear with zeal
I wanna harness the power of love
Ride endless waves of passion
Embrace the glory of each new dawn
And instill meaning in every moment
I wanna live without apology
Create infinite beauty all around me
Be open and honest and peaceful
And ignite a fire in every soul along the way
I wanna anchor my spirit with faith
While sailing through vast seas of time
Reveling in the compilations of wisdoms
And strengthen bonds of every heart I treasure

NATURE'S BLESSING

The clouds have settled in the field beyond
Becoming a mystic arena of dampened wishes
As the dandelions glisten stagnantly by the weight
Still and silent allowing the dew its due
Captivated by its sheer domineering presence
While the refracted light seems to slow time
Creating an elegant illusion of lifelessness
The rising dawn's pressures shift consummation
And gracefully the mist untwines its spell
As the penetrating rays reach through the density
Gradually spreading tendrils of warmth
Dissipating the droplets lingering upon the surfaces
A recession of the fog abandoning its kiss

THE TOLL

I believe it's true you give pieces of yourself away
To the people you fall in love with along the way
Fragments of your heart for the life that you shared
Maybe they are tokens offered to show that you cared
The light from your soul to brighten theirs when it's dark
Even the fires of your spirit to maintain the spark
It's a metaphysical exchange of our energies within
None of which is returned or reset when you must begin again
So you're starting anew while parts of you are left behind
Hostages of memories that may or may not be kind
But that's where they dwell now with those of our past
While we learn to accept things and move forward in contrast

FROM WITHIN

That longing within
pressing against your mind
Making you miss things
you've never really had
That rhythm within
echoing through your soul
Driving you to find something
even when you're blinded
That yearning within
beseeching a destination
Non-existent on any map
as it resides in another heart
That calling within
baritone voice without words
Urging you to listen
and heeding where to go
That desire within
caressing your spirit's core
Setting fires of passion
Burning trails to follow
That need within

Beckoning you to keep going
Stripping away fears
To push against the odds
That belief within
Consuming your every thought
As you hope and pray to attain
The treasure you have sought

OFF-KILTER

It's messy inside my mind right now
And I started wondering if my energy is too
The saying goes what you put forth is returned
So, if you give love you should get love
If you're not, then you shouldn't
But it seems to me that my vibes aren't equated
Not directly proportionate at all
Almost as though there's direct opposition
A force intent on rigging the echo
Twisting and contorting the backflow
While the rebounding energies knock me around
And it's making my thoughts jumble up
Concerned that I'm doing things wrong
As I'm unable to receive like for like
I give honesty yet I get lies
I give loyalty and instead I get betrayal
I try to encourage growth and expansion
But I'm doled out stagnation and restraint
My spirit is waning to the point of retreat
The risks just don't offer much hope
That my vibrational output is properly aligned

Feels like everything is out of sync
An untuned instrument just making noise
There's no beauty to rejoice in
No sense of abundance to be grateful for
Only a hodgepodge of purposeless chaos
Generating doubts and weakening my soul

LIVING DEATH

Sometimes events in life hit us hard
With battles that hurt us deeply
Taking us through treacherous paths
We never fathomed treading
The pains that we encounter
Tear the marrow from our bones
Weakening our struggling spirit
Shattering the hope in our hearts
And casting us into darkness
Leaving us with despair and grief
Under the heavy weights of loss
Drowning our minds in sorrow
From the endless tears we shed
The light within us fading out
As emptiness consumes our soul
While the focus steals the future
Swallowing us by the shadows
Of trauma that can't be changed
Allowing the past to overtake us
And feeling we're left with nothing
Surrendering ourselves to brokenness

Attempting to numb out the heartache
As our world crumbles to pieces
Unable to rise above the torment
Until we're buried alive to suffocate alone
Every thought stricken by demise
Defeated and helpless we die inside
Agonizing over what's gone

DUST IN THEIR WAKE

Some people will never see themselves the way they project
They use and absorb the light of others for survival
Because on their own they excrete nothing but darkness
Making the people around them simply a means to an end
Putting on an entrancing show for everyone to see
But if you look closer it becomes evident it's just reflective
Seeing past the charade isn't easy if you're drained
When it's your very own energy being used against you
It becomes a thirst-quenching mirage as you die in the desert
Making you so parched there's no choice but to chase the dream
They manipulate with distractions that warp time
Until they've managed to take every available resource
And leave you behind as they're drawn like a moth to another
Spitting you out as a random particle emitted by a black hole

ONGOING

As the last wisps of winter whip through
felling all that's lifeless to the surface;
You won't see the beauty autumn once offered
just the bleak and bland coverage of death.
While the essential cycle of transformation
makes way for new growth from every end;
And the decay nourishes seedlings of spring
allowing flourishment to rise once again.
All life graced with fortitude and strength
to outlast the blistering heats of summer;
Then traverse majestically into the next season
enduring every perilous stage of existence.

MAKING WAY

Have you ever felt hollowed out; as though the core of you were gone
Or that you're so empty there's nothing left that makes any sense?
I've allowed people into my life who have drained me
By taking and taking with their perpetual selfishness
Leaving me unreplenished in numb indifference
A wavering vessel angry at my own nature
As I gave and gave until a void is all that remained
Yet by the suffering of loss after loss I've realized
That even though I felt nothing was there
Light had taken up residence claiming the space within me
And slowly as it eradicated the heavy darkness shadowing my mind
I could see clearly that it had always been present just downcast
So now I'm free to make way and renew my spirits shine
And revel in the reemergence of who I truly am.

RESOLUTE FAITH

We are all born into sin
That's how humanity came into existence
With no man bearing strictly saintly qualities
As there is evil levied within each choice
And learning to balance ourselves
According to the chosen alignment
Is an effort we struggle with every moment
Retaining all the light we can harbor
While expelling the darkness that intrudes
Is a construct all souls should apply
To avoid leaning into foul temptations
That are more often easily attainable
I would rather surrender to glory
Even if it leaves me standing alone
As everyone's spiritual journey is unique
I cannot cast judgement on others
But pray they sway onto atonement
Instead of stumbling through misdirection
Led by ill will and hollow hatred
Heaven can be a state of being for the life of your spirit

And I prefer mine to glow with love
Radiating a positive aura inside and out
As I walk with faithful resolution through this life.

JUST BECAUSE

There's no way to keep track
Of how many times over the years I've asked why
As though probing deeper will help
When the simple question
Already has an answer even when left unvoiced
If things weren't meant to change
They wouldn't
If people were destined to stay
They would
When everything seems to fall out of balance
There's a reason
Whether you see it or not at the time
And why is revealed in the journey
Because if we all remained where we were
We'd never get anywhere near
Where we should be.

ACCREDITATION

I end up giving credit when it's not truly due
That's how I get taken advantage of
By picking up the slack to level things out
Misplacing attributes I've inadvertently overlaid
Making the union more than their efforts imply
And I'm not certain how to refrain from my nature
Can a giver be any other way?
But it's imperative I stop disillusioning myself
Taking off the glamour of emotions
And view with reason their participation level
Are they giving as much as I'm putting in?
Is their stride keeping pace with mine?
Or am I towing the line for us both?
Because if I am then they're not worth it
I don't want to pull someone with me
I deserve much more than dead weight
The journey of a loving union isn't a one-sided venture
It should be a haven against the world
Both striving to thrive together
Building a mutual bond of honor, love and faith

Without blurred lines of intention
It should interlock their lives into one another
Undoubtably proof positive
That while I'm giving everything that I am
They are undeniably doing the same.

OVERCAST

Someone complimented my blue eyes today
and even though it took me off-guard
I managed to smile and thank them for their kindness.
Lately when I've looked into the mirror
all I've seen are gray eyes staring back
so, I felt compelled to look for myself after their comment.
Still I saw gray
but couldn't help wondering
how they could see one color and me another?
I know that the ocean appears blue
even though water itself is clear.
And that murky sediments can make things look darker;
depth can also change the shade seen.
It's all to do with light and its reflections
into our own eyes that interpret and correlate color.
But why can I not see what they do?
Are mine clouded?
Perhaps I should just be grateful
they can see them in a beautiful blue hue
and that my eyes to the outside world are reflecting

a lovely tone of vibrancy and life.
While I'm too caught up in my own depths
to see past the shadows
I gaze through.

BEHIND THE SHEEN

Ours minds can play tricks upon us
Glossing over the view
Shielding reality out of sight at times
While serving up fantasies latched to lies
To bend our wills unwittingly into acceptance
And then shattering the mirage as revelations break
Belief is a strange enchantment
Difficult to decipher
Or even when its necessary to step away
But every illusion contains fallacies
Shifty sheens occurring within the glamorous façade
Awareness of the discrepancies opens a rift
Offering a glimpse
Between what's true verses imaginary
So be attentive to the wavering energies
To avoid getting swept away by fleeting emotions
Woven webs of worthless words
Designed to ensnare with false hopes
Stay attuned to who you are
And always wary of the inexplicable

For in every doubt that lingers upon the surface
Triggered by deceptions
There is a truth that lies in wait

STAYING FOCUSED

I've realized that in the throes of loneliness
My selfishness has overshadowed my blessings
And even though I am grateful beyond measure for my children
It's not the same meaningful bond I crave
Yet they are my anchor to the present love I have
While my heart continues to cry out
For one that's absent
And fear may not exist to fill that void
For now, I have to ground my focus and rise above the yearning
Staying mindful to those who depend on me to thrive
As this isn't my time; its theirs
Gifted into my life
Teaching me how to cherish the time at hand
Since it only lasts for a moment
Because before I know it their youth will pass by just like the years
And even though the echo within me is silent to others
I still hear it
Whispering softly
One day, just not today
And it soothes the wariness of my spirit with hope
That time can always bring new possibilities into the future

But you can't get it back once it passes
So, it reminds me to appreciate what matters now
That they are enough to keep me centered
As I've been entrusted to keep them safe while they grow
And to wrap myself up into their loving little souls' embrace.

FINITE

There are many undeniable aspects of life
Yet the most revering one is that everything dies
Knowing that fact humbles your hopes
But certainly, saddens your heart
When you see living paralleled to the truth of death
You can learn to accept the beauty of its existence
And acknowledge the glory of its light against the darkness
The contrast of its rebellious state while thriving temporarily against
the odds
Knowing all the while that the end relentlessly approaches
Yet we cling to denial as though it were breath
Replacing the purity of our purpose with a battle
That bears a meaningless wager to defy the absolution of mortality
We must relinquish the notion of forever
And realize there is a finite number of beats in our hearts
Quit trying to escape the present with the past or the future
By simply reveling in the time you have at hand.

RESURGENT

She reads the scattered stars strung upon the sky as constellations
Poetic proof this universe isn't random
Just as the burning words the pour out of her mind
Show that the energy of her spirit is alive
They could not come from a pale corpse without breath
But from an entity shrouded in pain
One who has felt the tainted blade of life
And still bleeds from the infliction
Seeping the sentiments of those struggles out in ink
Scribbling them across the pages
To fuel an inner desire of resurrecting a spark of hope
Not only for herself but for others who have felt reduced to dust
Adrift
As if disappearing into the backdrop of the vast expanse
Was but one scene ending
Behind the heavy curtains cloaking of illusive invisibility
And time will pass
Bringing awareness not all darkness is evil
Often, it's a role of renewal
A spiritual shifting of perception
As she phases through the resurgence

Like the moon reflecting its cycles of available light
When the sun touches its surface to yield a majestic glow against the night
Not everything must be seen to hold its place in space
Even if only a mere sliver shines
It remains whole

DIVISIBILITY

We tend to subdivide our personalities
Sticking things into categories and separating them from the whole
Sealing certain parts off into their own room
By erecting barriers within ourselves instead of unifying the
variations
Its as though we quarantine segments of our true natures
Hiding them away from the world
Fearing judgement for who we truly are
Not only from people we don't know but more from those we do
Without even considering
They too probably hold similar insecurities
Concealing their own secret selves tucked safely away and out of sight
As everyone tries to fit into an ambiguously molded notion
Of what's perceived as acceptable
It only serves to deduct value from unique aspects
Subtracting differences as if they were inconsequential
Setting each further apart from the other
Until falsely deeming yourself an outcast
Falling victim to a contorted defense mechanism
Because denial changes nothing except your ability to be real

And hinders anyone's acceptance of you
When you refuse to even belong to yourself

NOT ALL LOVE LASTS

You don't realize how powerless you are
Against the things you dare to love
Until their loss weighs heavy upon you
Bringing you face to face with the reality
That sacrifices had been made
To maintain what was prioritized
Over the rational that it was not yours
And never really was all along
Only a fictitious possession of the heart
That leaves a gaping hole with its departure
As you grieve the absence of its presence
And try to reclaim all you gave up by holding on
To one that didn't

LUMINOUS

Her aura appeared iridescent
As the setting sun cast its rays upon her
And every color of the rainbow shimmered
Like she was a multifaceted gemstone
Rare and beautiful
And even as the night had risen
Silently under the darkness of a new moon
Her inner radiance continued to outshine
Even the closest stars in the sky
Because when he looked at her
With those tawny eyes filled with love
That's how she felt

HYPE CAN BE JUST THAT

Most often the glimpses we view of other people's lives
Are simply the highlights they've segmented out for show
Fragments of their story not an all-encompassing truth
But precious moments of time set out for display
And commonly meant to appease the attention they seek
Or distract outsiders from questioning their life choices
By eliciting emotional responses of praise or envy
As what's visible lays out the assumption of progress
That they'd prefer others see as opposed to what's real
Leaving out all the behind the scenes footage
That would dissuade everyone from watching the show
Since the trailer's intent is to captivate an audience
Willing them to focus only on the grandiose dots they've presented
Instead of acknowledging the lives in the design have flaws
Just as much; if not more, as everyone else does
So, no accurate comparison can be made from false depictions
Within those illuminated fairytale webs they weave
When it could all just be their hollow insides reaching out
Attempting to fill a void that's ever-present in their life
While trying to convince everyone these moments define them

As whole, or happy, or better than, or as a changed person
Silently praying no one notices how truly hopeless they feel
Because then they may have to face it themselves

YOU THINK I'D LEARN

I know that I place too much value
Into the words other people express
But only because I know that mine
Are not spoken without intention
Most times I end up feeling
I may be the only one who does that
While others merely use them as bait
To reel in what they want and then let the line go
Even if I'm still attached to the hook
They didn't care enough to be real
So why would they care if I'm hurt
You'd think I would learn to stop listening
Apparently its hard to unhear people
Or to not trust them if you love them
Maybe I should try using them as they do
But I can't bring myself to be someone I'm not
If I did, I'd be no better than they were

ALTERING COURSE

With words…
I can create light in the darkness
Turning shadows into a lover's tender caress
Or even dispel the weariness from a broken spirit
By imbuing hope into their heart
Its possible to shift ones focus from joy over to pain
Just bringing up reminders of past betrayal and deceits
By simply saying yes, I could open a door that was closed
Offering a chance to reignite a forgone flame
If I chose to do so I could mince a clear mind with worry
Inlaying doubts where one holds faith
Its easy generating a storm to overcast sunny skies
Through a thunderous barrage of anxiety
I can reach beyond limits that don't exist
Since the depths of imagination are boundless
Should I toss a rock into calm waters
Just to watch the ripples cascade outward into chaos
With quiet I could drown every noise
While I wait for another to hear my soul song
Or I may want to disintegrate time into ashes
And just let it tick by unsubstantially

A few words can ignite an unquenchable passion
Leaving one breathless and craving more
Or like some, I could add subterfuge to pure intentions with greed
And live a lie just to avoid being lonely
Maybe it was me disillusioning myself with blind trust
By negating words that had no follow through
If I blow out the candles, substituting wishes for reality
Perhaps I overlooked the untruths to live in the dream
I have found I can forecast ends that haven't even begun
Because I already know all things do
Its not impossible to dismantle years of memories
Just with a murmured goodbye
And just as quickly jolt back into a recurrent thought left unhealed
To keep a wound bleeding out within you
I could lay my ear upon your chest
Listening to the beat of your heart speak to me
Learning how to master the instillation of belief
Imbedding the toxins from the thorns of roses
And then watch the victim totter out of the garden
With their words echoing thru the deafening rage
Yet there are no words keeping one tied to such a road of peril
When desire yields a heading to alter my compass

EVOLVE

Changing
That's the battle
The continual struggle
Between feeling and knowing
And each time you reach a summit
One of many transitional points
You'll realize
Everything contributed a pulse
Each energy created a ripple
To disrupt the calm of comfort
Helping to loosen the stagnancy
And aid the shift of transformation
To accept the new horizon
Moving you through the becoming
Into the truths of purpose
For your wellbeing

TRADE OF THE MISGUIDING

No loving heart should accept
Someone who generates blurry intentions
For there's no positive outcome that will arise
From the painful impact of gameplay
So be aware that when they test the line
It's a ploy to gauge how much maneuverability they can levy in
Positioning themselves into power
To hamper any willingness of sacrificing the connection
By hazing the perception of its worth
When really, they plan to stay detached
Leaving the other to grapple through the misnomers of truth
While they take advantage of the fabricated opportunity
To utilize their target as a mode of convenience
While most every word and action have holes in their validity
And no full sense of security accompanies them
They subtly undermine your integrity
Simultaneously providing enough support to keep you guessing
While they reel in attentions
Not only from you but wherever else they choose to get it
Using things you enjoy as an avenue for deception
And you're misled by their inclusive appreciation to your pastimes

But it's just to sidetrack the sights
away from them having unaccountable time
There's so may delusional tools they employ to sidestep trust
While they traipse around behind your back
Hoping you never catch on to their bullshit

WHILE YOU'RE HERE

Nothing that breathes will conquer mortality
But those that truly live
Can create things that will linger on infinitely
The legacy you leave behind when you fade
Will shine light on the memory of your existence
So, I implore you to find your passion
And pour every ounce of energy into it
All the blood, sweat and tears will triumph
Over the anxieties brought by fear and doubt
Do not let time erase you
While you're here
Make it count

PHASING FLARE

My sights drifted upon a draft of light
No other eye could see but me
I absorbed its every photonic trigger
While I was caught up in the energy field
That blinded me even from time
And the array seemed to caress my spirit
As it began to lapse through the impulsive stage
Stifling me with the heated intensity
Of an internal eruption unparalleled to any other
This cycle drew out exponentially too long
Exceeding beyond its intended momentary presence
Through years of densely woven wavelengths
Until I had lost sight of myself
While the decay of toxic stagnancy
Set up charges with interspersed detonations
As it lingered far longer than a mere solar flare should
Upon the sun

TRANSCENDING

Everything that occurs in this world of energy and dust is divinely
orchestrated
Even when things don't make sense there are reasons paths become
castrated.
We are led through fork, curves and tunnels for beyond our sight lies
a maze
And this labyrinth of life can be confusing leaving us feeling we're
trapped in a haze.
But the point is to see the many obstacles in the form of lessons to be
learned
By developing our senses and use the wisdoms to ascend levels as
they're earned.
Our souls are transfixed inside form, yet the spirit can move about
at will
There's a key to structure a harmonious balance while we're
submissive to the wheel.
Yielding to hope through each orphic cycle to keep reaching for the
highest tier
Destiny interconnect multiple pathways of ease and of suffering past
our tears.

And you could be the smartest person alive but still possess an untrained soul
If the focus was gathering knowledge without applying growth to your being as a whole.
The uniqueness of our capabilities lays dormant until its awoken in each
Though some never experience their potential if they block reception from reach.
The mysteries of our universe unveil in your faith as you acknowledge all you are
And accept any pains as an integral element necessary in your transformation as a star.

IN THE WASTELAND

It's odd how the mind can generate such grandeur
Around a concept that's triggered by emotion
And weave an illusion that conceals the unappealing
While tethering you to incomplete falsehoods
As the manifestation overtakes personal perceptions
Weakening the ability to determine what's real
And strengthen the power of the mirage
Using every hopeful desire within you against you
Weighing you down with sand masquerading as water
Your willing to consume to quench the ever-growing thirst
But the grainy burdens heavily stunt progression and growth
Settling you into a wasteland of wishful thinking
And you succumb to the stagnancy
Under flourished and wilting helplessly in the barrenness

PAMELA JEFFS

BIOGRAPHY

Pamela Jeffs is an author and occasional poet living in Queensland, Australia with her husband and two daughters. She is a member of the Queensland Writers' Centre and has had numerous short fiction pieces published in recent national and international anthologies. Her debut collection of short stories titled *'Red Hour and Other Strange Tales'* was released in March 2018. For further information, visit her at www.pamelajeffs.com or on Facebook at @pamelajeffsauthor.

SCARS

I saw my brother in a dream,
With heart and mind in disarray.
He wore the scars of his war,
Painted in shades of grey.

I saw a letter that he wrote,
The words already fading.
Asking where everyone had gone,
His memories degrading.

I woke with tears in my eyes,
My brother, he was taken.
Death in life, is life in death—
Us left behind, forsaken.

So I farewell bad memories,
Say goodbye to the toll.
I'll watch for him in other dreams,
My real brother—the man Bipolar stole.

C.L. WILLIAMS

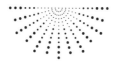

BIOGRAPHY

C.L. Williams is a multi-genre author from central Virginia. His most recent poetry book *The Paradox Complex* currently averages a five-star rating on Amazon. In addition to poetry, C.L. Williams has released one novel, four novellas, and has made several appearances in anthologies and magazines. When not writing, C.L. Williams is reading and sharing the works of other independent authors.

You can find more about this author on Facebook, Twitter, and Instagram.

BE MYSELF AGAIN

I can't get everything from my mind to my heart
But I'll do all that I can to make it never fall apart
I know deep down I need to go to who I used to be
Because this person you see I feel isn't me
All of my feelings, they're becoming mechanical
Everything of my being, is starting to only feel chemical

If I only knew then
Today I want to be myself again
I never would've took that road
The one that took me far from home
But I only want you to see
I want to become the old me

The world around me has helped me sensitize
The people close to me helped me empathize
Helping me be who I need to become
Sharing myself and losing my numb
All of my feelings, are feeling less mechanical
My entire being, is starting to feel less chemical

If I only knew then
Today I want to be myself again
I never would've took that road
The one that took me far from home
But I only want you to see
I want to become the old me

Here I stand before you a better being
As I feel all of my burdens finally freeing

I didn't know back then
Today I would be myself again
I took that road but I'm a better man
Back home and better I stand
Here I am for you to see
That you see a better me

EYE OF THE STORM

Here I stand in the eye of the storm
A changed man, ready to reform
The rain that falls, we face it everyday
No matter how heavy the burden may weigh
Storms wipe many moments away
So it's a new beginning, starting today

I face the rain to see the sun
I stand here cold, I will not run
I'm willing to deal with the worst
I will go in the storm fully submersed
Now I stand here stronger than before
As I stand in the eye of the storm

I know it's a burden but I'm not here to run
Even if the pain is like a bullet from a gun
Storm turned flood, it's heavy on my head
I remain here for those who've already bled
I shall let the storm wipe everything away
Have a new beginning, tomorrow or today

I face the rain to see the sun
I stand here cold, I will not run
I'm willing to deal with the worst
I will go in the storm fully submersed
Now I stand here stronger than before
As I stand in the eye of the storm

The storm has finished running its course
I am still standing here the stronger force
I remained in the storm, fragile as a vine
The storm has passed and now I see sunshine
The storm came in wiped a great deal away
But here is our genesis, it begins today

I face the rain to see the sun
I stand here cold, I will not run
I'm willing to deal with the worst
I will go in the storm fully submersed
Now I stand here stronger than before
As I stand in the eye of the storm

GUILT

Nightmares of my day, another sleepless night
The guilt does this to me, story of my life
Do something wrong, my conscience begins to eat
Picks at my soul and it makes me weak
The moment has passed I cannot apologize
The guilt takes me and possesses my mind
The moment is there and it's stuck on replay
Thinking of everything and everyone I betrayed
The guilt inside of me makes me want to hide
Because deep down the guilt is eating me alive

HOMECOMING

The maker called, he's ready for me to come home
I just wanted you, you'll never be alone
I have much to tell you, I'm not guaranteed tomorrow
The maker has called, my time here is now borrowed
One thing I must tell you, always believe
I know it will be difficult since I'm about to leave
But you have to be strong, at least for the others
All of the family, even your sisters and brothers
If I only have time to say one thing, I know it would be
No matter what, I don't want you to cry for me
I know you'll want to since my time here is through
You'll understand better when the maker is ready for you
So I say this, do not cry because my time here is done
Because my life isn't over, it's only just begun

REMISSION

My soul has been in starvation
So I come to you seeking salvation
I don't know if this is my preemption
I'm only here asking for redemption
I only want to rid of my anguish
So I ask, please make this vanquish
I want to put my life in the clear
I want my pain to disappear

I want to restart the ignition
Show the world my own definition
To be able to follow my own intuition
I only want to put my pain in remission

I need to have my mind vindicated
Enter this new life fully translated
Time of my past, it's time to omit
Enter this change I must commit
It's time to see myself ascent
Rid myself of all this torment
I want to put my life in the clear

I want my pain to disappear

I want to restart the ignition
Show the world my own definition
To be able to follow my own intuition
I only want to put my pain in remission

HAIKUS

Collect

My words can connect
Maybe even intersect
The thoughts I collect

Haiku 299

A sky that turned grey
As the clouds water the Earth
And we call it rain

Into the Unknown

A challenge ahead
It's into the deep unknown
Let's see what's ahead

My Place

My place in this world

I am still searching for it
Infinite journey

Sounds of Nature

Whisper of the wind
A whistle as it glides by
The sounds of nature

Sunset

Clouds over the sky
As the sun begins to set
And darkness will rise

The Cure

The world is diseased
And I am making the cure
Saving you from you

Untitled

Overcoming odds
The role of the underdog
I'll fight to survive

All I Have

I am all I have
Only one to have my back
Only one I trust

Captivate

Captivating words
But my thoughts can be frantic
Leaving you breathless

ROWAN THALIA

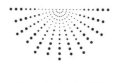

BIOGRAPHY

Rowan Thalia is a poet and RH Paranormal novelist. She wrote her first poem at age sixteen after finding and losing her first love. Her love of poetry and short stories developed into a drive to write novels when she first participated in a novel writing club at the school where she teaches. Her debut series, the Keepers of the Talisman, began releasing in February 2019 through DSP. She has eight books currently in the works.

Though she will forever be a New Orleans girl at heart, she now lives in Washington state with her husband and two children. Prior to settling down, Rowan's zest for life and culture brought on many adventures. She has lived in four states in the United States and has also had the great joy of teaching abroad.

If she isn't hard at work writing her next dangerously exquisite novel, you might find her reading, teaching, camping, or indulging in her secret vice- watching B-rated horror flicks.

INTENSITY

Darkness falls
    Intensity
    Engulfs me

Taking me into
    Distant waters.

Here and there
    My body bounces
    Streaming, effortless

On his countless waves.

LOSING TO INTENSITY

Intensity turns
His eyes toward me.
Cool waters
Rush through my body.

Thousands of raindrops
Fall on hot skin.
Intensity calls
And I must follow.

Mountains are moved
Boundaries are broken
How much further must I go
Before my return is lost

THAT SUMMER

Summer nights
Long ago
He held her close
Safe from harm

Demons danced
At her door
Yet he held tight
Banned the evil

Summer days
Long ago
They loved, laughed
Danced through a dream

The world sat
Watching from afar
As two lovers held
Onto all they knew

THIS PLACE

Here I am
I feel as if I have been
Here before
Maybe I have

My surroundings
Disgust me
Dark, Dingy, hellish place
So close to being home

Look at me
See that I have been
Dirty, tainted, hurting
Ask me where I've been

This place, this home
This was built
By hands no
Other than my own

Read my mind

Tell me whether
I like it here
This home that is no home

The writing on the walls
Clearly states
What evils lie inside
The heart of an angel

THE SWEET SURRENDER

Stranger of mine
Come sit by the fire
Leave the world behind
Let me yield to you

Of only for a few hours
I would have you
Yield yourself to me
Let me yield to you

Gather me into your arms
Let me feel the strength
Of your body against
My own sweet temple

Search my skin
Explore my secrets
Take me into your world
And then beyond

I surrender to you

My soul and my body
Take it lover, for it is
No longer under my control

Ride me into distant places
On your stallion manhood
Make me weep with desire
Then die in my own passion

ABSOLUTION

Have you ever felt
Wasted, tired
Lonely, wanting
Good, so do I

It's as if
My life has
A will
Of its own

Taking me off
In the opposite direction
From where
I wish to be

Into a well
Of emptiness I fall
It echoes the
Loneliness of my soul

I lay at the bottom

Looking toward the sky
Hoping to catch
A glimpse of his face

For in that face
I could find
Absolution
And be freed

ME AND MYSELF

Standing outside myself
Realizing what is there
I am me, yet again
It is so nice to reunite myself

Dwelling in the past
Old relationships slip away
I am here to guide myself
Cleanse my soul

Hurting no more
Feeling so renewed
I am glad I found myself
Before she gave up on me

Standing beside myself
I shake my own hand
You have done well, my dear
Happiness seems inevitable

Loving life, living again

I and me laugh together
Sharing the sunshine
After the storm

Standing inside myself
I hold me in my arms
I love you myself
It's so good to be home

ALLAZO

I searched the world over
Only to find nothing
Then I gave up on me
Only to become nothing

I let the world take over
Only hoping to find something
Then I lost myself searching
Only trying to get something

I changed my life
Only wanting to go somewhere
Then I became myself
Only still going somewhere

I cheated on myself
Only to realize anything
Then I became what I hated
Only to find anything

I stopped myself
Only to change everything
Then I found myself
Only to be everything

CHARLES REIS

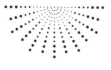

BIOGRAPHY

Charles Reis was born and raised in Coventry, Rhode Island, but currently lives in West Warwick. He graduated from the University of Rhode Island with a BA in English Literature in 2012, and currently he works as a museum tour guide. Additional works of his have appeared in "One Night in Salem," "Trembling with Fear: Year 1," and "Encounters with the Paranormal Volume 4." You can find him on Facebook, LinkedIn, and Instagram.

LIFE BROKEN

My young life has been broken
Abuse is my life's token
I have been lied to by all
And this has led to my fall

Living on causes me pain
Now I feel like I'm insane
What have I done to get this?
There will be no loving bliss

When awake or fast asleep
I feel that my life is cheap
I hate the sound of life's bell
Someone help me I'm in hell

SHADOW OF EDEN

The gates were destroyed by fire,
Started by mankind's desire.
The valley was devoid of life,
The death caused by a blood-soaked knife.
Lust,
Pride,
Hate,
Greed,
They all come from Adam's seed.
In the Shadow of Eden,
As the apple rots.
It poisons our veins.
So we are all dead,
Now send us to Hell.

COLD

I feel so cold,
Inside I'm dead
No one to keep me warm
No one to keep me red

My heart shivers
These frozen tears
I can't show my true life
I can't show my true tears

Alone in ice
Loss on my mind
Your warmth I cannot see
Your warmth I cannot find

Darkness on me
Sun gone away
I wish that you could help
I wish that you could stay

APOCALYPSE

Fiery death rains from the skies
Buildings crumble before my eyes
Dead bodies are covered with flies
Peace on Earth was just lies

Anarchy now rules the street
Cops are the criminals
Parents are the children
Priests are the devils
Society is dying right at my feet

The rivers turn into blood
And bullets piling up in the mud
Violence comes like a flood
My friends killed in cold blood

It's something I always feared
Countries are a catacomb
Cities are a tomb
Homes are a coffin
The end is here

BORN AGAIN

Salvation,
It isn't in my reach
Heaven,
It's only in my dreams
God,
I don't understand him
Hell,
Am I already there?

Hear my cry?
Is God a terrible lie?
But what if it's all true?
Can I throw my life away?
Kneel down and go God's way?
Destroy all that I am?
Am I the disease?
Or is it Christianity?
Who is really born again?

HATE/LOVE

I once believed in it
with you,
But now I slit your wrist

The one thing that I've learned
by you,
Is love will get you burned

Love's a terrible lie
from you,
So tonight you will die

All the insults you say
to me,
Sent all my love away

I embrace my own hate
from me,
I see this as my fate

The hate is what I'll feed
within me,
It's time to make you bleed

TWISTED LOVE

I cannot believe that I fell in love with you,
I want you to know that all things I say is true.
Like that I love you so much that I'll kill someone,
I don't care if it's for revenge or just for fun.
Just show me the person you will want to see dead,
Then I will show my love by turning the place red.

I love you so much I'll do anything for you,
Just as long you know everything I say is true.
Like that I love you so much myself I will kill,
I will die just for you even against my will.
This is my dying love for you and it is true,
Just remember that I'll do anything for you.

DATURA LILY

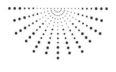

BIOGRAPHY

There is no doubt in the fortitude this writer presents her readers, unbinding them to conventional thought and shifting their internalized hurts into shared experiences. She connects with them at a point of pain through lose, injustice and betrayal, then bridges the expanse of emptiness they leave with every scribed emotion to counter the void of feeling alone.

She has a breath of ink squalling over the pages melding cloudy skies to raging thoughts. Using her tears and blood that seep into words forcing things to light that darkness tries to hide. While she weathers storms of change in her own life tethered by roots of hope that sustain her will and give her tainted petals even deeper beauty as they bloom in the adversities of life.

RISE OVER DEMISE

I found that when faced with the pain of betrayal
Everything else around me faded from view
Overpowering my thoughts and turning them dark
With a pitch the consumed every light
I began to see through the torturous patterns
As I bleed the words upon paper in ink
And each time I reread them listening aloud
To the roiling damage I felt within me
To the anguish weakening my spirits strength
And to the rise of demise I'd allowed upon my soul
I was dwelling in the chambers of my heart
Every beat relinquishing the residuals of hope
While I slid deeper into the tombs of despair
Until I realized that I alone had to rise
Out of the feelings and out of the thoughts
To look upon them as a separate entity
Not as who I was
And not allow them to overthrow the glory of life
But expel them as experiences of growth
Not harbor them as dominate masters
That could snuffer my existence

A QUE FROM DESCENT

Remaining stuck
in a time warp of dooming thoughts
becomes a perilous journey
of wading through the darkness
While everything seems to spiral
out of falsely taken consention
forcing you deeper and deeper
into an abyss of tormenting pain
And it takes every shred of strength
left scattered about within
to cling onto a remote hope
that merely flickers like a dying light
When the walls are crashing in
to bury you beneath the burdens
as the disparaging memories continue
to mercilessly bombard your soul
And as the weight becomes too heavy
to bear alone anymore
that's the que to reach out
and pray another takes your hand

Someone who hears your spirit screaming
between every laboring breath
willing to help you rise above descension
and retake a hold on life

RUNNING PARALLEL

Some people are never content...not truly
Yet they say they are
With empty words of appeasement
All the while shifting effort into alternate ventures
Plotting another course to run parallel
Searching for something
Anything they can find to fill the void
Inside their heart
Without ever acknowledging
That what's missing cannot be found in another
They hold the key
While continuing to flee
Away from the primary issue
Evading themselves
Until they come full circle and accept
That no matter much someone else loves you
It will never be enough
To maintain the light self-love supplies
To keep you present
Grateful for what you have

And happy with who you are
Without it you'll always be running beside yourself

CONCEPTUAL FUEL

Some inner thoughts are better left unkindled
In a world that's slipping further away from grace
Not everything that crosses the mind should come to light
To keep darkness from rule
They should remain in the recesses where they lurk
We all possess that place within where questionable things dwell
And its prominence ebbs and flows in accordance
To how much girth its given when it spikes an impulse
Chances are that in times of pain we tend to let them linger
Enveloping ourselves in foul bitterness
To justify the adage of an eye for eye will ease our discontent
But it won't soothe or heal anything
What it will do is shroud the acceptance of change
And hinder the ability to generate positive energy
Everything is levied upon a balance of good and evil
We learn to strengthen the side we choose to conceptually fuel
Developing a framework for our mind's moral navigation
So, by dispelling the negatives before they reach fruition
We gravitate toward hope that radiates harmony
The spiritual resource needed to counter sins weight
Freeing ourselves from burdens that are too much to bear

UN-UPHELD

I thought we were in this together
Bonding our lives into our life
But you kept instilling distance
Tottering perilously between want and have
As selfish immaturity outweighed honor
Casting no value on moral conviction
By imparting continual treachery
Between every breath while crushing hope
Beneath the empty vows you spoke
And all the deceitful actions
Threw sand upon the fire we had built
Dousing the flames of desire with doubt
Sending up trailing sparks
To burn out in the air above
Like a field of fireflies losing their light
Everything just went dark
And my marred heart sunk in silence
Among the ashes of what was once our love

TO COME UNDONE

Uncage me from the walls I'm confined within
And lock me down in the essence of your soul
Touch me as if time would cease if you didn't
And show me what it feels like to be yearned
Release my inhibitions and let me roar to life
Make me believe that my love is a worthy cause
And not a wasted adventure that just yields pain
Awaken the passionate beast that sleeps in you
Entrust my heart to beat in sync with yours
Bring me to my knees as we revel in raw desire
While caressing the battered spirits in us both
Healing each other's energies on a primal level
And bonding us together until we breathe as one
Melt my inner core by igniting a deeply fueled fire
With a penetrating heat so hot we're never cold again
Allowing me to come undone naked and exposed

SHADOW SELF

The shadow of my soul is willful
Demanding an unencumbered presence
Spitefully repelling the light within
And refuses to conjoin with its primary
It's the harbinger of my pain and anger
Stricken to exude its resentments
Outpouring the sulkiness upon my spirit
And dampening the hope
My radiant self strives for
Every day it threatens dominion
A black hole in the fabric of my being
A barely leashed particle of destruction
Readying to overthrow its fractal carrier
Unless I solidify the energies
Decreasing the auric turbulence
With a strong current of divinity
Until the cast of darkness fades out
Into shredded rifts of disillusion
That no longer contain enough power
To preside on the throne as my ruler

ETCHINGS OF MEMORY

You cannot be haunted by the living
Only the memories that keep them present
And as difficult as it sounds
Escape comes when they are forgotten
When you ease into the acceptance of solitude
Refocusing attentions to ideals that matter
And allow the vacant space time to reabsorb
Blending into the background more effortlessly
Perishing the remnants that keep it on the forefront
Continuing to fuel current thoughts of emptiness
Stop restricting your power by giving it to them
Cease the recall that glorifies good times
While omitting the negatives
As that overshadows the truth of the absence
And underscores your own sense of worth
Phase out the past routines connecting you
Developing new passions that ignite your spirit
Always remember time is too valuable
To let someone who doesn't deserve it remain in the light
Set them aside just as they chose to do

Tuck the memories deep within the past's graveyard
Realign your purpose and don't falter with a back step
Tripping over a stone marker etched in your heart

SELF INFLICTION

I awoke to these words whispering through my mind
And it felt as though every tear that befell
Was chiming a tune of forgiveness
I could never say aloud
But seemed to sing to him…
Time has unraveled wisdoms
Revealing truths, I was once blinded to
Opening my eyes to revelations that ache bone deep now
Since my actions belied my heart
I awake at night hearing her voice in my dreams
Feeling as though her love still calls out to my soul
I should have been what she needed
The man she believed me to be
But instead I let her down and lost her
Not having her in my life is my punishment
The karmic restitution for my selfishness
Left stricken with the heavy knowledge of what I had
And the painful acceptance I can never get it back
While I'm stuck somewhere I should have never been
Without her

All because of my foolishness
Now only able to cling to the memories of our past
Even though she will never know
I will cherish what she gave me for a lifetime
As my true heart song will always sing for her

STOP THE REELING

Its been said that the person your mind wanders to
Is where your heart is
And its not meant to be there anymore
Which only confirms the loop hasn't broken
Only that I've got to find a way
To stop these feelings
Of being caught in a vicious tail spin
And even though I ejected from the craft
There's part of me left behind in there
Still reeling in the emotions
Is this the aftermath of surrendering?
Of foolishly giving my whole heart to him
Maybe once he broke it
I never really got all of it back
There's something missing and I don't feel whole

...Will I ever be?

ALL IN FEIGN

Seems a pointless venture seeking to find
Something as fleeting as love
It isn't tangible enough to grasp
Only a concept that can be feigned
Regardless of what you felt
The portrayed reflections of action
Like mist in a mirror
Unsubjected to actual existence nor containment
Yet the most sought after figmentation
As though hope alone
Could make it real and even still
No matter how much you want it to be
All it really is
Is the sum of intentions
Intertwining another's with your own
But fickle hearts weave painful illusions
And false proclamations fade out the imagery
Leaving nothing in the end
Because it wasn't truly there at all

PERSEVERE

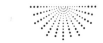

Life doesn't slow down on demand
Doesn't give extents of space when things are a mess
Or let you catch your breath and figure things out
Its up to you to wade through the during
To muddle by at times the best you can
Pull back in moments to reevaluate the strategy
And learn how to restructure on the go
Because it will keep going even after you fall
Not ending like chess at checkmate
The board is always in play
You've got to find your strength to continue
Beyond every doubt that's thrown at you
Or over obstacles that block your sights
You may not see clearly at every turn
And sometimes might not see a way at all
But maintaining your perseverance, your will to live
Is the key to navigating a journey
Where you are the primary lifeline of your timeline
So even though it won't wait
Don't you dare quit on it

WHERE WE ARE ONE

If the only place we are allowed to be
Is all we have left of each other
Then that is where our souls shall meet
For it's the only way to feel your touch
Or taste your lips on mine
And savor the warmth as we entwine
Relishing in the vast space between time
Where all the restrictions fade away
And there's no concept that we are lost
As the we that was still exists here
Making it the only option to be with you
And the only place I yearn to be
With every waking moment spent in longing
For the drifting that brings us together
Where we are one as we once were

ONCE UPON A PAST

A TRUE connection is more than mere words
And the loss of LOVE run deep
Two lives disentwining DOESN'T make the sun shine brighter
Sometimes its just their futures that SIMPLY change course
Forcing each to FADE off in separate ways
Pulling AWAY from the united life they built
BUT the heart still beats for them
The feel of their missing touch LINGERS upon the skin
Even though they're no longer WITHIN reach
Sometimes the ONES closest seem to hurt us the most
Still the seasons will cycle as every SOUL evolves
Vows no longer BINDING them together
Traces of presence flicker out into MEMORY
As the shifting from endearments TO silence sets in
While thoughts of ANOTHER in their arms becomes retching
But day by day an aching HEART heals
From senseless betrayals THAT tore it all apart
ONCE upon a past
Allowing self-worth to BEAT out the pitfall of depression
Knowing self-respect is essential to move ALONG into acceptance

That wanting them by your SIDE doesn't mean they're meant to stay
And it may be hard to release them from THEIR promises tied to the
hopes you had
But it's for your OWN peace that you must

YOU AND I

For you are like the moon and I the sea
Sharing an inter aesthetic currency
Both your presence and absence profoundly affect me
I rise to levels you push me to reach
And then recede back ever so subtly
You create ripples and wakes upon my tranquility
Passively forcing the shifting tides with your energy
As though I alone am unable with any urgency
To flow my own way freely
Like it is you that gives me life
Choosing how I should be
Weighting me under your will
Without any emotion I can see
Setting my currents tone within your own incongruency
But I don't need you to exude a sense of calm
Nor to prompt a rage of calamity
By pressuring me into incivility
I alone am aware of my every intricacy
For I exist just as you, as my own capable entity
Neither of us truly in tune to the other, no destiny for unity
So, while I may waver beneath the sky

I never come close enough to thee
Whether I submit to your whims or wager a storm to flee
And regardless of the cycling phases it's time we both agree
That you and I are nothing more
Than a merciless passing fancy

QUIET COMPANY

Do you ever crave company
But silence at the same time
It's like needing comfort
Yet not wanting to talk about anything
You just require someone's presence
Without interference into your thoughts
That feeling that they are with you
Is enough to warm your heart
And not add any extra stress
Or pressure to explain yourself
When you have no words
To make it all make sense
It's simply their quiet companionship
That can make you feel normal
Instead of isolated from humanity
While your mind processes
Whatever's weighing in on you
With more ease
Because you're less alone
In the comingling of energy

BLUE WATERS

I'm learning to tread the waters
Over the cresting tides washing in
That knock my breath out now and then
When memories still surface
From under the waves that took us down
Beneath your silent indiscretions
Leaving my mind as adrift
As my heart feels now
Wondering if there was ever a time with you
That anything at all was real
Or was everything we were
Merely docked upon your lies
Time's design is failing me
To let the past of you just fade away
Instead the dredging currents seem to deepen
Without any viable reason day to day
And while I grapple over thoughts of love that linger
Like a lifelines floating tether
Connecting me to someone
Who's no longer here to weather
The storms that come and go

Or anything else with me
I know that the sea of emotion within
Is simply settling itself back in
After a churning disruption ripped through
Touching everything just to vanish into the blue

WHEN IT HURTS

Strength is not the absence of emotion
It lays in the fact that every feeling
You have beating in your heart
Has relevance
Serving a purpose that's impactful
Of accepting the core of who you are
When life is jovial, then rejoice
But when things hurt you can learn to heal
Its alright to admit something affected you
There's no reason to hide your humanity
Even if some moments lean heavily into pain
Or imply vulnerability
Those don't look like simple weaknesses
It shows that you have roots
They show you to be real
Shining light onto what you value
And nothing is stronger testament
Of character
Than being able to acknowledge
That losing something you love
Can bring you to your knees

TO HEAL ALONE

Sitting here through the misty morning hours
Delving into my mind missteps
And overanalyzing where it all went wrong
I seal myself off from people
While the tormenting memories cycle around
As their judgement will not ease me
Oddly enough this is just how I heal
Buts it's the during they don't understand
I already know what they think so why hear it
What I don't need is further debasement
Downplaying how I think or shaming what I feel
Considering its not the first journey
Through the darkness of unrequited love or loss
No one can walk my path but me
And somethings we are meant to do alone
Seeking out our own truth from within
Transforming the pain or despair into strength
It's a way for me to reign in past impacts
An inner tactile reminiscence of sorts
Reevaluating ideals and realigning my heart
Establishing a more solid sense of self

After a hurt struck so deep it depletes you
It's the allowance of time to identify mistakes
And overcome future relapse to those transgressions
Trying my best to ward off triggers until they fade
So that I may reawaken hope and resurface in the light

GARETH BARSBY

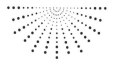

BIOGRAPHY

Gareth Barsby is a writer of prose and poetry, which he uses to explore many bizarre and unusual worlds and the characters that inhabit them, and even illustrates them from time to time. He is a graduate of the University of Chester, where he studied Creative Writing and Journalism, and has had his work published in several anthologies. He has also had a novel, Reindeer, published in 2016, and currently runs a blog where he frequently shares illustrated poems and short stories, which can be found at myweirdwriting.-wordpress.com. He also has a Facebook page which can be found at https://www.facebook.com/myweirdwriting/

THE CROCODILE AND THE SNAKE

A crocodile and a snake,
Who were husband and wife,
Lay in bed, talking about,
How they were bored of life.
The snake, she said, 'Everything,
Has gotten so routine,
I need something to do we haven't done,
Something to see we haven't seen.'
'We should pop down to a pub,'
Said the croc, 'and go be merry!'
'But nobody would talk to us,
They find us both too scary.'
'Maybe we could plan a day trip,
And walk around the zoo!'
'If we went there,' replied the snake,
'They'd cage me and you!'
'When it's hot, let's go to the beach,
And sunbathe on the sand!'
'But all the humans will scream and run,
Don't you understand?'
The croc thought and thought and then he said,

'You know what would be fun?
If we went up to the humans,
And scared them, every one!
'We jump out of the shadows,
We leap out on the street,
We terrify the humans,
And really make them shriek!'
And that's what they did in the morning,
She hissed and he did roar,
Just to scare the humans,
Which was not a chore,
The snake giggled as she heard the screams,
'This is fun, it's true,
Now I remember,
Why I married you!'

THE WISE OLD TREE

The wise old tree upon the hill,
Wants to speak, but never will,
Because of what gives him a chill:
No-one comes to see him.
He has plenty he could say,
He could help you find your way,
But he remains silent all the day,
For no-one comes to see him,
He's surrounded by beasts and birds,
He's not too far from fields with herds,
But they don't listen to his words,
And no human comes to see him,
Nobody wants to hear him speak,
For they see him as a freak,
Trees with faces make them shriek,
So no-one comes to see him.

A SUPERVILLAIN'S SHARK

A supervillain sat in his lair,
A place sinister and dark,
He said, 'I'll find the hero,
And feed him to my shark!'
The shark tapped on the glass of her tank,
For she had a question:
'Must I eat the hero?
He'll give me indigestion.'
Said the supervillain: 'Silence!
That's what you must do,
Listen to your master,
Or I'll make soup out of you!'
This made the shark so angry,
She said, 'I'll be frank,
I don't like being your pet.'
So she burst out of her tank.
She slapped the villain across the face,
With her fins and tail,
He was out for the count,
So she sent him to jail,

So rest easy, citizens,
You need no longer fear,
Supervillains attacking you;
The hero shark is here!

D.S. DURDEN

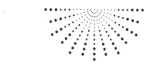

BIOGRAPHY

D.S. Durden is an android residing primarily in the swamps of Floridaland. D.S. Durden shares a home with a menagerie of quadruped creatures, many of which trace their origins back to Earth. He enjoys writing semi-biographical sci-fi and fantasy stories but has occasionally found himself on stages performing spoken word poetry. Reveling in his ability to move members of the audience to tears, D.S. Durden specializes in angsty strings of words that showcase the aftermath of lost love and self-destruction. He also likes space a lot.

GOOD INTENTIONS

Empty is the wandering heart. Hollow is the searching soul. Sobering is the inevitable tragedies.

There are devils in these waters. These creeks and streams that I've crossed to make it home. The rushing tides crashed against my body to peel away my demons. To drown them in the waves, I held them under to make them suffer. I smiled at their decay. I felt accomplishment in their banishment.

And it's true that I let the flames lick my skin before I stepped into the water. I hate who you made me. But it wasn't even your fault. But I guess I had to learn self-discipline somehow.

In truth, I learned a lot from you. In all honesty, I find it needless to regret. You still remain to be a source of inspiration. And as much as I hated how you'd tell me to go find happiness in another's arms, I believed too deeply. I held fast to a ship I refused to believe had already sunk.

I'm sorry I made you hurt me. I hope you can release the guilt I left in your hands when I begged you to stay. When both our hearts were too broken to even beat properly. And I'm sorry I brought out the worst in us. I tried. I had good intentions. And I tried.

SAVIOR

I want to save you from yourself. I want to lift the veil that traps you
in the void. I want to raise you from the pit that pulls you deep into
the depths. A droid without a purpose. Decaying, anxious corpus.
I wish I could make it okay. And if I may, say that I want to make
everything alright. I hate when we fight. It breaks my heart. Well, for a
start—what's left of it. What hasn't cracked and crumbled. Blackened
and stumbled out from my sternum.
I left my fear of defeat when I packed my bags. I don't fear death. I
only worry of the backlash. The recoil. Slashed and scattered across
the crash. The wavelengths that resonate from fate that cut one's
strengths. Into halves. Halves of halves. That reduce the bull to a calf.
I hurt for those around me. Cast aside and pale as a blizzard's last,
weakened flurry. The ones lost out to sea. My heart forgot what it was
to worry, about itself. And I'm sorry for all that I'm not. And believe
me—I fought.
Breathing, hearts beating. I'm terrified to wake up to the cold. The
unbecoming, empty vessel. I can't stress this enough. The barren
house that we wrestle with the idea of. The concept that we'll return
to a home that feels less welcoming.
You deserve a savior, but I can't save me from myself.

MELTDOWN

Dust...is settling on the glass. And yet again, you haven't done what I asked. What I begged. What I needed. I pleaded for you to handle things. I thought you could see things through but apparently you sought something different. I fought for you. I spoke for you. But I've since learned that I should no longer get choked for you.

Toxic meltdown, breakdown. Seared on the edges and cracked until every perfect surface was drowned in the confusion of abrasions and bustings of trust and tormented from dusk til dawn.

I need a minute. Because none of this really computes. None of it. Look, whatever you're looking for in me? I...don't have. Not for you, at least. Don't...take it personal. It's just the whole thing feels wrong. And quite frankly you're not strong enough to handle what you're seeking anyway.

SPIRALING

Welcome to a point in time that seems strangely like that other point in time a year ago. With the screaming, and the yelling, and the forgetting what's most important.

Welcome to that point in time that seems to continuously resonate and bounce back. Making itself apparent just often enough that it's not forgotten.

Welcome to feeling hopeless. Terrified. Lost. Yet...strangely enlightened in a way that makes you feel sick.

It's a sick scenario that replays itself far more often than it should. Although, really, it should never. Not. Ever. But there it goes. Round and around, weaving ever so tighter to the center until it swallows everything up into a sort of blackhole. Black...death. The plague. A plague, that seeps into my skin. To rot my mind until there's nothing left desirable.

I'm...dying inside. I'm...crying for acceptance. And no, I don't need forgiveness, because I'm not the one claiming lies as truths. I fear that you'll never be proud of the creature I'll bloom into because you'll never fathom that I can exist outside of the mold. All of this—all of it! Has really gotten so old. And you'll twist and contort my words until they're nothing like what you were actually told.

You...you make it difficult to not run away again. To not make a stand like I did a year ago. To prove that I'm strong enough to pack my shit and leave when I reach my limit. But the worst thing here is the fact that the whole point of that is to prove something...
Something that just keeps spiraling right past your head.

MURDER, MURDER

Flying on the wings of crows.
Murder, murder . . .
The ascension into madness.
I fell from such great heights, compressed into sadness.
***
My bones shone when I crumbled to the pavement.
Bereavement.
Disbelieving, deceiving.
How much I was reminiscing in all that I was missing.
***
When dreams gave birth to nightmares and the fields turned to
scorched earth.
Pairs of lairs made for heirs, glares pointed to theirs like daggers
meant to stagger.
***
I disemboweled all the vowels to howl from an old tower.
Built from the walls I have made, when flesh met blade.
***
But even then, I have never been so zen.
Than when the crows' strife brought me back to life.

Murder, murder . . .
Rising from the nether, I quite fancy my new feathers.

YOUNG DEVIL

Tell me, young devil. When did you lose your voice? It used to echo across the canyons, causing landslides of snow and dust, tumbling rocks down over all that was below. Used to make tidal waves that would crash against the shores, sweeping all away that wasn't tied down.

Tell me, young devil. When did the girl in you blossom into a man? The strong-willed girl who wouldn't take "no" for an answer. You grew into a silent man. You grew into a doormat for unworthy people.

Tell me, young devil. It was not the man who killed you, was it? It was the world who drove that stake through your heart so deep. It was the world that tried to define you for everything you weren't, and the world that made you feel ashamed for everything that you were.

Tell me, young devil. Does your heart still beat? Does it still pulse against that iron nail that's pierced your fierce heart? Even if you rose from your disheveled grave, could you learn to stand again? Could your feet even support all that is you?

Young devil...have you become too much for this world?

Young devil...this world never deserved you.

PERFECT EVIL INCARNATE

Before the venom
He was a beast
When it entered his veins
He became a monster

Dressed in black and grey
With a perfect smile
Framed by a five o'clock shadow
He's perfect evil incarnate

He does everything better than me
He fights, he manipulates, he demands
Through conquest and conceit
Blood and deceit

He's perfect evil incarnate
Consuming my soul
Til nothing is left
I fall victim to his concern

Maybe I'm projecting
Maybe I'm not worth his protecting
Nowadays I've hated myself more than ever before
He's perfect evil incarnate

SUPERNOVA OF THE LOST LOVER

It's always been difficult to start these things. It's hard to find the right words to convey what I want to say. It often happens like meteors. A brilliant flash that streaks across the sky just to burn out and vanish. But oh, for that moment of light—it was fine!

But oh, you were once mine.

I longed to sit beneath the nighttime landscape with you. Darling, you had a way about you. That made the stars not seem so distant. Like I could see galaxies in your eyes and constellations in your freckles.

And I could never give you the world. Because, well. It'd be ridiculous to give you yourself.

I love you. More than I could ever express in words alone. Despite a thousand miles, you used to be merely a phone call away. But that's all changed. Life now just seems so deranged. And now, I fear to say that we are estranged.

I will never forget. Nor will I regret. But I will not return. Never the matter how much you may burn, I will allow you to become a star in its final stages. Blossoming into a beautiful supernova that blasts away all of its layers to eventually collapse into a blackhole.

But I'd prefer you not. I'd prefer you make like I have. May your heart not become a hunk of coal. May you develop the ability to love again.

May you find compatibility and stability in someone who loves you the way I used to.

I doubt anybody will love you the same as I still do. Not in this way. For I have let go, despite making quite a show, I thought I had come to know. But I was wrong. Nevertheless, I have found redemption and finally learned how to be strong.

More than anything, I hope you do, too.

THE WITCH AND THE TRAVELER

In the eyes of a Traveler, the Witch saw a perfect sunrise within. A horizon built not of fires and roses, but mossy greens that knows his foggy greys. Latent cries from an overgrown glen, echoes that shatter all the creations of men.

Believed to be each other's soulmate, the years melted away as if wax from a lit candle. But her love became too much to handle and from the Traveler's lips dripped words she came to hate.

The façade would fall and turn to something that would sicken as the entity she loved betrays her. The Witch's heart withers like trees stricken by the onslaught of winter. The pain brought by a fractured, flawed identity reduce her confessions to a slur.

Rotten fingers cascade across broken flesh as a bottomless pit digests his threshold. It's been said that she's undead but she's merely holding onto an empty chasm where a heart should be. With each beat of his own he made his way toward being alone.

A love like cancer. Heartbeats like the pounding of fists on a barricade, demanding of an answer. Petrification of a union once pure, with heavy emotional debts left unpaid and unsure.

Yet despite all the romance a darkness crept beneath the skin. The Witch will no longer allow him another chance. She knows now, that to be so forgiving is not always harmless.

The Witch inquires, "is it a sin to love in this way?" To obsess and confess the pain and stress, molding a future from clay? She savored his words with every last breath of her labored lungs, but what was once soft like silk erupted into briars.

It's horrific. The relationship, to be specific. Might I add, the end result even more so. With a stab between his ribs, she twisted the blade and a path down to hell they made. And as they fell, she mouthed the words, "I'm sorry, but you must go."

Before she lay dead she felt remorse not for the words she said, but because of how things had to transpire. With the works of magic and wire, the Witch would soon stitch herself back together. Dismantling every bone and every tendon—a crone she is not, a grave no place for her to end in. Far from perfection, she penned the lyrics to her own resurrection.

SPACEDUST

Bring me home to the moon and the sky. Where the galaxies danced until they died and the stars didn't seem so distant. Where death and rebirth is the same thing and limitations are few and far between. Bring me home to the cosmos I used to know and love. Where the goddess made herself known to the people and helped them understand without punishment. Where the only thing that brought pain upon your soul was bringing pain upon others. Where hell was truly deserved but not the end of the journey. Where heaven was freedom and love.

I'd like to understand how anything could ever hurt me. Since my body is made from the bits forged from the burning core of a star. When my very being holds the remnants of such an immense force. I'd like to know why I feel so forsaken. So lost.

MATTHEW M. MONTELIONE

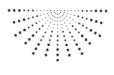

BIOGRAPHY

Matthew M. Montelione is a horror writer born and raised on Long Island in New York. His stories have been published in *Quoth the Raven: A Contemporary Reimagining of the Works of Edgar Allan Poe*, *Thuggish Itch: Devilish*, and other titles. Matthew is also an American Revolution historian who focuses on the local experiences of Loyalists on Long Island. His work on the subject has been published in *Long Island History Journal* and *Journal of the American Revolution*. Find him on Twitter at SpiritGuildBook.

THE WATERFALL

"Take me to the river!"
The duckling said with a smile.
"I cannot my dear,"
replied the mother,
"for it is rapid and runs wild,
we would surely drown."

"But why drown?"
asked the yellow-feathered baby.
"Because the waterfall of earth
will come and blow us both
downward, and we would drown."

"Where does the waterfall lead then?"
he asked.

"It leads to the sea,
it flows through the wind.
It sprinkles the sky
with its rocky grin.

It leads to the ends of the world.
But you must see;"
whispered the mother (like the breeze),
"that all paths lead you back to me."

THE SIXTH OF JUNE

The weathered gray stone was cold,
Like the remains of her young soul.
Seventeen years of life and love,
Grasped by Death in wartime sorrow.

She bloomed but withered in the Spring,
The sixth of June when songbirds sang.
Her father had pledged to the Crown,
Her rebel spouse worth many pounds.

Neither saved her from the dark ground.

RED

Time undefined swells my soul red,
It has spread to the tips of me.

Red like our blood mingled as one,
Red like skies of the sleeping sun.

Red like the rivers of Hell run,
Into my heart on a night breeze.

THE DEVIL OF EARTH

Eager was the bat to fly,
Parched was the sandman of time,
Barren were the trees,
Oaks, birches, and thick pines.

Lonely were the ghosts,
Who never really died,
Tans hues washed the grass,
That was green in the past.

Dried were the waterbeds,
That once held the ocean,
The Devil of Earth sat bloated,
Draped upon the domed sky.

THE WOLFMAN

Blue moon waxed bright and full,
The fortune teller's pull,
Instilled loud fears in hearts,
Minds much too dark to rot.

In agony, alone,
The doomed man cursed his bones,
Though his love was quite strong,
It did not quell Hell's wrong.

In solitude he swayed,
In the deep night he played,
Yet silver struck his head,
And made sure he was dead.

OAK TREE CHAGRIN

A gnarled oak tree lent its leaves
To the river's lucid grin.
They were to be taken to the waterfall
And drowned deep within.

The water smiled as the oak was deceived
Again, again, and again.
And as the stars dreamed the old oak tree
Gained another knot in its back.

KAREN JEFFERS-TRACY

Karen Jeffers-Tracy is a climate science educator for the two-thirds of us who are non-scientists, kinesthetic learning styles, and liberal arts majors. She believes all people deserve to understand enough about climate science to contribute to the necessary transition; recognize the manipulations of the denier campaign; and support positive solutions to the climate crisis, when they are proposed. She facilitates her local writing group, where the group support provides "whatever you need to succeed." Her writing is inspired by her continual fascination with the complexity of human beings, the difficulties in relationships, and how even people who love each other can drive each other crazy.

Karen is an enthusiastic researcher, science supporter, loving mother and grandmother. She is dedicated to ending fossil fuel emissions, reversing global warming and ensuring the survival of human civilization. Her articles appear as The KarenClimate Corner, science delivered in bite-sized bits.

You can connect with her at KarenClimate.blogspot.com, or on Facebook at Fairborn Writers Connection.

LOVE-O-METER

I will always love you.
I love you even now.
At thirty-seven percent less
Since your screaming fit.
My heart is not indestructible.
Shuddering blows, repeated shocks
Diminish my heart's capacity to love
You.
Or maybe, love at all.
Before yesterday,
I loved you
at sixty percent.
Less thirty-seven percent
leaves my love at
thirty-seven point eight.
And since love is life
I refuse to lose any more.
I'll wall myself off
Build a shield of steel
Cut cord upon cord
Until no tie binds

Pull from my body each barb
Smooth all scars
So you will be
Sixty-two point two
percent free of me
As I will be of you.

GERRY SARNAT

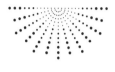

BIOGRAPHY

Gerry Sarnat MD's won the Poetry in the Arts First Place Award plus the Dorfman Prize; has been nominated for Pushcarts plus Best of the Net Awards; authored HOMELESS CHRONICLES (2010), Disputes (2012), 17s (2014) and Melting The Ice King (2016); and is widely published including recently by New Ulster, Gargoyle, Stanford, Oberlin, Wesleyan, Johns Hopkins, Virginia Commonwealth, Harvard, University of Edinburgh, Columbia, Brown, Main Street Rag, American Journal Of Poetry, Poetry Quarterly, New Delta Review, Brooklyn Review, Los Angeles Review of Books, San Francisco Magazine, New York Times. Mount Analogue selected KADDISH for distribution nationwide Inauguration Day. Poetry was chosen for a 50th Harvard reunion Dylan symposium. Gerry's been married since 1969 with three kids, five grandsons and looking forward to future granddaughters.

To learn more, visit gerardsarnat.com

WHO WANTS TO BE BORN HERE?

LLC Inc.'s Group Priorities
    Imperfect, we work
    hard on our meditation/
    medicine practices.

Craving [Maybe] Meditation
    Top of mind check-in
    that flash-scratches love's surface,
    then counting out breaths

I can only get
    to six before real itches
    begin to distract.

Muscle Building
    Good mornings sitting
    on our floor cushions could well
    tenderize my heart.

. . .

F[r]iction
Weightless suffering –
part of the stream – possibly
float free 'stead of sink?

Life Coach
Too busy earning
a living as a young man,
now a grandfather

I've all the time in
the world to splash in creek with
my kids' sons -- 'til don't.

You've Come A Long Way, Baby
Zeyde[1] gave me cubes
of sugar when he plopped two
right in hot coffee.

Coach offers grandkids
sips of luke tea with pine nuts
plus sprigs of fresh mint.

---

1. grandfather in Yiddish

JANUS UP THE YIN-YANG

Different Strokes
　　Don't go to a beach
　　where all the lifeguards have lost
　　the knack how to swim.

Diet
　　Shrunk to occupy
　　less space, I try to become
　　other indulgent.

YOUR ROYAL HEINOUS YANG

Presidential Pod
　　Between you and me
　　how can we prove our odd chief
　　is now Putin's stooge?

DHARMA

Hunt

    Miles away – disguised
    Buddha radiates light, almost
    levitates – I wake.

EQ

    Two's company, more
    a crowd? Learn how to mature,
    connect manysomes.

Middle Path

    Holding two opposed
    concepts in mind at same time
    for enhanced function

wisdom impetus
    to mix endogenous with
    outside stimulus

. . .

Buddhism/ Ecstasy
　let go attachments/ deepen
　love, intimacies.
　Gerard Sarnat

Family Jewels
　Called America's
　Mayor then Pathologic
　Lawyer — Trump's Rudy.

The light that never
　knew how to turn off: I do
　miss Robin Williams.

Blessed Be
　It is time for me
　to quit complaining about
　just everything.

On The Noble Eightfold Path
　My gravy-train job's
　woodland parkkeeper, growing
　organic veggies.

GALINA TREFIL

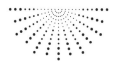

BIOGRAPHY

Galina Trefil, author of *The Incomplete Ones: A Tale of Slavery* and *A Cape for Kali*, is a novelist specializing in women's, minority, and disabled rights. She is soon to debut two new books, *Low Caste Girl*, a collection of Romani-American feminist stories and *One Cell in Corcoran*, a book dedicated to the gladiator fighting victims of the notorious California prison. Her work has appeared in *Neurology Now*, *UnBound Emagazine*, *The Guardian*, *Tikkun*, *Romea.CZ*, *Jewcy*, *Jewrotica*, *Telegram Magazine*, *Ink Drift Magazine*, *The Dissident Voice*, *Open Road Review*, and the anthologies Flock: *The Journey*, *First Love*, *Sea of Secrets*, and *Suspense Unimagined*.

THOSE WHO SLEEP IN DUST

My heart is pounding like it cannot stop
And my eyes keep rolling on up to that clock
Time's supposed to be flying, but it's just not
Each day just feels like Sisyphus' rock
Perhaps, in the darkness, I should take new stock
Perhaps it would help me adjust to the shock

Of whether or not caged birds really sing
Or if they can fly once someone's clipped their wings
And, if push comes to shove, they'll fly if they must
But, when they do, will they crash or glide to the dust
And, when they are buried, can they dig themselves out
These are the things I sit and worry about

If you stare long enough, you can learn to see
But no one who looks has ever seen me
So I sit in the darkness and I dream of trees
Of how good it feels to lie in the leaves
And I wonder how long before that can come to be
And I wonder how long before I can be free

Stare into black and think of your chores
To sit here and sit and then sit some more
Memorize the walls and study the floor
And dream of the voice you heard long before
And ache for the face you love to your core
And ache for the day when they come through your door

And whether or not this caged bird is singing
Silent replies are what this life keeps bringing
I've denied desire—I've controlled every lust
Still my only choice is to live in the dust
And whether or not I can dig myself out
This is the thing I sit and worry about

And my heart is pounding—it will not stop
And my eyes keep on twitching on up to that clock
Time's supposed to be flying and flying a lot
I suppose it just flies like Sisyphus' rock
Perhaps, in the darkness, I can rewrite this plot
For some choose surrender, but I do not

I hear every tick of the clock when it rings
And I've come to want so very few things
Now I did what I had to—I've done all I must
Please, God, keep faith with those sleeping in dust
And I'll have back the life I am dreaming about
Because I know someday I will get out

Beyond any singing, I will learn to shout
These are the days I am dreaming about
And I'll sleep by my lover and not in the dust
And value the time when a bird learns to trust

CUTTING THE FLOWER

To the vampire who just won't let go
To the violent one who now disowns
To the drunk whose fists will wander
To the one who just will stand there
As you bleed into your despair
And your fingers yearn to reach that phone….
But you can't, so you live it, and live it alone

These are our parents
Who can be surprised
We weren't always smiling
We weren't always wise
Who would be shocked
We've messed up our lives
Just like our parents
Don't let us be our parents

To the father slamming against the wall
To the mother who won't ever call
To the one who calls you names so much

And makes you fear to be touched
Until you say enough's enough
Stand on a cliff and wait to fall
These are the ones who break us all

To the one you'll love until you break
To the one who will just take and take
To the one whose love makes you defiled
And makes you parent instead of child
And you fear what report was just filed
And you wish you weren't your parents' mistake….
For they deserve better and it's all for their sake

We have just fled
Now we will be free
We'll cut that flower
Right at the stem
You'll wake up you
And I'll wake up me
We won't ever awaken
And find ourselves them

To the one who makes you hide in a closet
To the one you makes you say, "Don't lose it!"
And, "Oh, my God—I think I lost it!"
She who never read you Green Eggs and Ham
And made you say, "Son of Sam, I am."
And the father who would never stop it
And whose number you crumple when it goes in your pocket

These are our parents
And no one's surprised
That we now love
But we still despise
No one is shocked

We've messed up our lives
To not be our parents
We will not be our parents

SHOES MADE OF LEATHER

I'm sorry I don't say much
I'm just not sure what to say
It seems I'm looking down forever
It's good my shoes are made of leather
I've got a long walk today

I didn't mean to do it
Whatever I know I did
Your accusations and your screaming
God, you sure can be demeaning
All in front of the kids

I think I guess I loved you
Once upon way back when
At least, I guess I gotta think so
Because all that I know
I can't love you now
If I didn't then

I'm sorry that I touched you
I thought you wanted me to

Now I'll go and shut my damn mouth
Now I'll go and sit there outside
Like you want me to do

And I'm sorry I don't touch you
I don't know how to fake
I keep on looking in my mirror
When did I get this much older?
I thought we met yesterday

Now I think I guess I loved you
Once upon way back when
At least, I guess I gotta think so
Because all that I know
I can't love you now
If I didn't then

And now I told you that I loved you
Christ, why can't you calm down?
God, I sure do hate this damn house
And I sure do hate your damn eyes
That follow me around town

And I think I guess I loved you
Once upon way back when
At least, I know I've told myself so
Because all that I know
I can't take you now
Even if I could then

Why is it that we go on?
Well, I guess it depends
Maybe I like the derision
And all your superstition
I'll love you to the end

I'm sorry I don't say much
I'm just not sure what to say
It seems I'm looking down forever
Why'd I buy shoes made of leather?
I'll sit right here today

GABRIELLA BALCOM

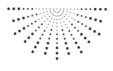

BIOGRAPHY

Gabriella Balcom lives in the lone-star state with her children. Her family includes three dogs that think they're human and are convinced they rule the roost (they do part of the time), and two cats that could talk your ears off (they're claiming they're the real rulers, and proving it more than the dogs would care to admit). She has a soft spot in her heart for other states and countries she's either lived in, traveled to, or dreams of visiting one day. She believes wonderful people and beautiful places exist everywhere.

Gabriella describes herself as a lifelong reader, loves writing, and sometimes thinks she was born with a book in her hands. Her background is in psychology and criminal justice, and she works full-time in a mental health field. She writes fantasy, horror/thriller, romance, children's stories, sci-fi, and about a variety of subjects. She likes traveling, music, good shows, photography, history, interesting tales of all sorts, plants, animals (especially dogs, cats, and wolves), and a lot more. Gabriella says she's a sucker for a great story and loves forests, mountains, and back roads which might lead who knows where. She has a weakness for lasagna, garlic bread, tacos, cheese, and chocolate, but not necessarily in that order. You can check out her author page at: https://m.facebook.com/GabriellaBalcom.lonestarauthor

TO THE LIARS WHO HURT US

Harm you have dealt me,
dung piled high so it'd be all I see.

Lies abound from thee—
awful slander to defame me.

I question. I tremble. In secret I cry.
Deep inside I ache. But I do not die.

I hide my anger. Sometimes I quake,
but I do not—*ever*—break.

They say time heals. I'm not there yet.
But in my mind I will not let rot set.

I have what you'll never have—the key,
the truth that will always set me free.

No matter your past lies—lying still—
you can't control the truth and free will.

Despite the horrible things you've done,
in the end I've already won.

LITTLE SQUIRREL

Spring is here,
the scampering,
playing time of year.
Nuts are plentiful today.
You don't need yet to
scrounge them away.
So, little squirrel I see,
we'll enjoy this day
together, you and me.

YOUR SPROUTS

Seeds lie dormant,
even in a heart.

It doesn't take much
for roots to start.

Thoughts are the sun,
actions the food.

Will your sprouts
be weeds or good?

MY CHILDREN

My children, the heart of me.
So strong, so intense my love,
it threatens to explode.
Can everyone not see?
A greater love could not be.

My children, the hope in me.
No matter the problems,
I continue going forward.
I find beauty in every sight.
The future awaits—bright.

My children, the strength in me.
Enemies may come, one or all,
but I fight on. I feel no fear.
Surrender I don't know—ever.
For you, I endure forever.

SAFE HAVEN

Everyone needs safe harbor,
shelter from the rain.
All of need a true haven,
a respite from deepest pain.

Christ can be our mooring.
He says, "Come. Believe."
He is our Redeemer,
and will never leave.

We all need protection
from life's slinging hail.
He is here to help us,
to ensure we not fail.

Loving Him may not
make for an easy way,
but we can gain strength
to live each day.

MY DEAR

The day we first met,
I was in a hurry—going fast.
You were in the library
when I entered, walking past.

Smiling, you said, "Hello."
Warmth I did see and hear.
Something about you
intrigued me—drew me near.

You seemed smart and interesting
and we talked and talked.
Similar habits and interests we had,
similar life's paths walked.

As days and weeks passed,
I grew to know you well.
We turned out to be soulmates.
This anyone could tell.

We've had our spats,

our worries, our woes.
But throughout everything,
we've been friends, not foes.

You're my best friend,
and I want you near.
You are the one in my life
I hold most dear.

FOREVER I AM THINE

When your tiny fingers
curled around mine,
I was no longer the same.
I became thine.

How could fingers so small
have a grip so great?
But I felt for you
I'd always been in wait.

My heart is yours.
My love I freely give you.
You were tiny then—adult now—
and I love you deeply. I do.

FIRE AND ICE

How can two opposing forces
comrades be?
Yet in me they are joined
in complete unity.

The hottest, deepest emotions
swirl around inside me,
along with the reverse—
icy restraint and clarity.

Calm. Storm.
Peace. Strife.
Fire and ice—
this is my life.

BLACK, YELLOW, RED, OR WHITE

Be you black, yellow, red or white,
everyone is equal in God's sight.

There should not prejudice be.
He loves you *and* He loves me.

Brother, sister, stranger, friend—
God is with us all to the end.

NO HAPPINESS, NO HOPE

Paint peeling
from gray walls.
A cheerless room,
even in daytime.
Dim yellow lights.
Murky darkness
night after night.
No visitors come,
not even her kids.

Eyes stinging,
feeling no hope,
the old woman
shuffles along.
Her nursing home
is the cheapest—
the most run-down.
Her heart aches.
So do her bones.

HAIKUS

Please go away now.
Some people only cause pain.
Life is much too short.

Something is nearby.
I can feel it watching me.
Should I stay or run?

Death's whisper I hear.
My remaining time is gone.
Still, the sun rises.

Everyone gets tired.
No one said life would hurt so.
Beside me, dogs bark.

IRENE FERRARO-SIVES

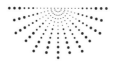

BIOGRAPHY

Irene Ferraro-Sives is a writer of poetry and stories. Her novella, *The Other Place in the Sea*, was published by Light Switch Press in November 2018. Her collection of stories, *Dressing at Guilder's* was published by The Write Deal some years ago. The Write Deal went out of business, so this collection is no longer available.

Irene was born in Brooklyn, NY. She has a BA in English from Brooklyn College of CUNY. Irene's interest in writing goes back to when she was a child and realized that words, even though they are only words, are powerful, and have the capacity to create or destroy. Irene uses words to create, not destroy. She wrote her first poem in 1963 about peace on earth. It was published in a children's magazine.

RUSHING RIVER

The street shimmered
In the summer heat.
The children ran in
Their own sweat
Trying to be cool.
Finally, someone opened
The fire hydrant.
The water gushed
Into the scorching
Heat, a rushing river
Pouring from thc heart.

JENNIFER CARR

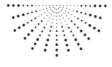

BIOGRAPHY

Jennifer Carr lives in Santa Fe, New Mexico with her partner and two children. She is an EMT, Firefighter, and emerging Poet. When Jennifer is not at the local hospital or firehouse, she spends every waking moment working on her poetry. Jennifer's Poetry has been published in several print publications including Triumph House Poetry with a Purpose and in several online publications. Her Haiku has most recently been published online in the Modern Haiku Section of the Organic journal 'Under the Basho.' Her Poetry has been in several National Exhibits including Poetry Leaves and Poetry Village. Jennifer loves to fly by her own wings and looks for any opportunity to soar to new heights! She can be found on Facebook at Jennifer Carr Munoz and on Twitter at JenniferCarr@Poetryhaiku13.

THE WARD

Scared to open
the heavy hospital door,
not knowing what my eyes
might or might not see
Shackles, chains?
Straight jackets, zip ties?
I guess that is only in the movies
for I saw none of that.
I saw her across the room
all alone
dressed in light blue paper scrubs
taking a bite of preselected food.
Slowly, steadily I walk towards her.
The hug was stronger than the strength
I thought she possessed at that time.
My shoulders back, head held high
not a tear shed
or a serious word spoken
I nodded constantly
acknowledging her small talk.
My left hand

slowly, stroking
over my lips
on purpose
left to right
right to left
like the wall clock
tick-tock
tick-tock
a secret hope
she would notice
the bare ring finger
no longer baring
a silver band.
Sadly,
I do not believe
she ever noticed
the missing ring.
Happily,
I do not believe
she ever noticed
the pinpoint pupils
peeping
small glimmer
lies behind
the thin white lines
still hope remains
giving me a new world
courage to break free
I can finally fly

THE MATADOR

Tired of fighting
life's bulls
one after another
please
take this red cape
away from me

BREAKING FREE

Years passed
till one day
courage found
to break free
from the cage
now a backbone
with wings

CARCINOGEN

My uncle is a cigarette burning
his smoke pollutes the air
ruining the lives of others.
He has me take a drag
off his shaft.
The sickness, the nicotine
fills my lungs.
My heart beats faster in fear.
I cry out in pain.
A pain he chooses not to hear.
He is a drug
he likes people to thrive on.
He does not know
the sickness he causes
nor does he know
people will dies from cancer -
his horrible disease.
I see the light shining
from the end of this cigarette -
it is my only hope.
The hope that

as this cigarette grows smaller,
he is fading away.
Finally,
I breathe the last of him
and stub the cigarette out
angrily
bitterly
full of hatred.
A pile of ashes
left to be stepped on.
One day he will be known
as a sick child abuser -
the day my cry will be heard
the day he will be punished
for all the lives he's polluted
On that day
there will be
no more tears
of sadness
only perfect joy

HAIKUS

entire world
in his backpack
thumb out

orange jumpsuit
another piece of trash
on the highway

bus stop
a needle in her pocket
day breaks

stand still
a traffic accident
in the headlights

tires
in a rut
anxiety

evening drive
two police officers
no mention of the accusations

SHAWN M. KLIMEK

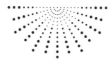

BIOGRAPHY

Shawn M. Klimek is a globetrotting, U.S. military spouse, creative writer and butler to a Maltese puppy. His stories and poems began appearing in e-zines and anthologies in 2017. The most recent of these include: "World War Four" and "Flash Fiction Addiction", by Zombie Pirate Publishing, "Curses & Cauldrons: Tiny Tales Vol. 1" by Blood Song Books, "Grumpy Old Gods", by Storm Dance Publications, and "Gold: The Best of Clarendon House Anthologies, Vol. 1, 2017/2018". Find books for purchase at *www.amazon.com/author/shawnmklimekauthor* or http://www.clarendonhousebooks.com/anthologics; find a comprehensive index of published works, including free online reads, at https://jotinthedark.blogspot.com; and follow his writing adventures on Facebook at http://www.facebook.com/shawnmklimekauthor.

POLLY WANTS A CRACKER

Polly wants a cracker, true
But wants some peanut butter, too!
A saltine has no small appeal,
But peanut butter makes a meal.
And while you're in the kitchen, dear,
Polly wouldn't mind a beer:
In establishments with class,
This comes inside a frosted glass,
Not plastic feeders in a cage
(Though any cold beer will assuage).
And rather than make several trips,
Could you bring potato chips?
Also, I think there was a smidge
Of onion-dip left in the fridge,
Beside the pizza wrapped in foil
Which would be such a shame to spoil,
So, bring that too, and—here I'm guessing,
Wouldn't that go well with dressing?
I'm also bored, if truth be told.
The news which lines my cage is old,

So, should you chance to pass beside
The remote control and TV guide,
You'll remedy another lack,
Killing two birds... *I take that back!*

BUGGED

'Cause he was small and had bug eyes,
His classmates used to pick on Grisham.
They called him names and said his size
And face were such no one could wish 'em.
It's bad enough kids criticize,
But did they really need to squish him?

DADDY'S JOB IS DANGEROUS

Daddy's job is dangerous, which should explain his fame.
Total strangers recognize him by the badge that bears his name.
We may watch him from a distance—never near while he's at toil,
Since, to his fore is scorching steel; beside him, boiling oil.
Though mobs may separate us, love is not deterred by that.
He simply waves his spatula or tips his paper hat.

WHO'LL LOVE YOU

Who'll love you when your beauty's blighted? I will!
Wrinkled, withered, weathered, whited? I will!
Vericosed and *cellulited*?
Darling, I will be delighted!
Though my gaze be uninvited,
I'll look on—and get excited!
Even when your beauty's blighted, I will!

Who'll love you when your mind is failing? I will!
Aged, *Alzheimered*, addled, ailing? I will!
Drooling, drooping, knuckles trailing,
Darling, there'll be no curtailing
My love, though your brain's derailing,
I'll find your drivel quite regaling!
Even when your mind is failing, I will!

Who'll love you when your fortune's faded? I will!
Pilfered! Plundered! Debt-Pervaded! I will!
Credit Damaged and Downgraded!
Darling, I remain persuaded

Any tax can be evaded.
As long as dimes are nickel-plated
Even when your fortune's faded, I will!

HEAVY IS THE HEAD THAT WEARS THE CROWN

"We are humbled," said her Highness,
"In the presence of our peasants;
"Rugged, rustic folk, who care not for renown!
"But how like soot the sovereign's soul
"Who would usurp her subject's role!
"Heavy is the head that wears the crown."

"Would any monarch but a mean one
"Stoop to grovel in a hovel?
"Sleep on straw? Or, burlap-booted, traipse through town?
"Although we're envious of their powers,
"It's the low-born's lot, not ours.
"Heavy is the head that wears the crown."

"A sovereign must have heart and sight!
"To want their plight is impolite!
"If we plow our people's plot, will not God frown?
"Such prideful deeds deserve derision!
"We're stouter stuff; of bolder vision!
"Heavy is the head that wears the crown!"

"I am but your lowly jester,
"Royal ruler," said the fooler—
"Yet I'm witness to the wisdom of the throne!
"Your heart's untouchable and fearless;
"As for sight, it's clear you're peerless.
"And your head in every weigh is like a stone."

SOMETIMES

Sometimes we can fashion fate;
Can ration hate;
Make passion wait;
Sometimes inspired/innate
Powers help us fashion fate:
Sometimes.

Sometimes, well meaning, I intend
A benign blend
Of sweetheart and adoring friend,
But dreams, they rend a dividend
Of sometimes more than I intend:
Sometimes.

Sometimes I just don't understand
Why, when the flames of love are fanned,
I'm always burned, while you get tanned.
You say a little love is grand,
But little things get out of hand:
Sometimes.

BABIES IN THE ATTIC

Babies in the attic?
Well, they're memories of me.
Yearnings of my yesteryears;
Who I'd hoped to be.

Through the keyhole, I can see them.
It's a sad, pathetic show.
They cry and beg for me to free them,
Chubby, tear-stained cheeks aglow.

Faded firemen, cobwebbed cowboys,
Doctors decked in dust like snow.
"I cannot let you out - not now, boys.
Only one of us can grow."

Babies in the attic:
My discarded infant dreams.
Childish childhood contemplations
With "someday maybe" themes.

In musty, melancholy corners

Of a cold, cerebral cage,
Orphaned infants, midget mourners
March in time, but never age.

Moth-eaten millionaires and mellowed,
Antiqued actors on the stage:
Like bound-in-leather books, whose yellowed
Edges frame an unread page.

Babies in the attic:
Rival heirs to destiny;
Bastard sons of boyhood visions,
Born to fail... instead of me.

THE SEAGULL

White linen wings stretched clothesline wide
O'er drape the wind, and footless, stride
Across the hollow, azure sky.
He peers down with a piercing eye
Moist with mystery and black.
An ancient, wrinkled face looks back.
The seagull soars, then swoops to shave
The foamy flotsam from the wave,
And swallows brine—yet bittersweet:
The swill contains a bit of meat!
At once, a jealous seagull nation
Erupts in cacophonous ovation,
Claps the air then tries to stand
A mile above the shining sand.
As white confetti screws the skies
Some imitate…some criticize.

JOSHUA LUPARDUS

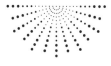

BIOGRAPHY

Joshua Lupardus is an American author and poet. He holds the degree of Master of Arts in Clinical Psychology and works for a local (southern Illinois- read as *not Chicago*) nonprofit agency to help people with serious mental illness live their best lives. He is an avid gardener, video gamer, and former champion powerlifter. You will usually find him procrastinating from his school work by writing for fun and drinking jasmine tea. His poem The Witches' Give Birth can be read in Darkling's Beasts and Brews: Poetry with a Drink on the Side by which was published by Lycan Velley Press.

THE HEART ON MY SHELF

She was beauty,
blonde, slender, pale.
A ghostly delight.

Everything she wanted,
everything she needed,
I gave to her.

But the one thing I wanted,
she gave to another.
Her very heart.

He cannot have it,
I won't let him.
I will take it for myself.

He wasn't there;
I would've been.
I would have never left her side.

I found her alone,

asleep in her bed.
She never even knew I was there.

The knife pierced
between her breasts.
My hands plunged into the wound.

I pulled it out,
her heart still beating.
It was mine, all mine, now.

And now it sits,
in the jar on my shelf.
Her heart beats only for me.

SYDNIE BEAUPRÉ

BIOGRAPHY

Sydnie Beaupré lives in her own imagination; a post-apocalyptic, zombie-inhabited world, where magical creatures and supernatural occurrences are simply the mundane. Outside of that, Sydnie can be found in Montreal, Quebec where she was born and raised. When she's not writing you can find her reading, playing the violin, singing, or spending time with her amazing friends and crazy family.

VINES

These vines choke me.
They climb up my crumbling body,
strangling me until there is no air left
in my choking, gasping, lungs

My foundation is weak.
It is falling apart because my bones
are tired, and the water damage from
years of neglect is taking its toll
Please, set fire to me.
Burn me down, so when I am nothing
but ashes, free of my vines,
flowers can grow in my memory,
my soul made anew.

SILENCE

The world is
Dark, and Bright,
Tranquil and Frightening
and it's been spinning out
of control for a long
Time.
We have been
Lied to, and lead down
Alleys that go nowhere,
And when we ask
"Where is justice?"
All we get is

S i l e n c e.

EMPTY

One day the sun didn't come out,
and when I asked you why, you *shrugged*.
When the air became hard to breathe,
I asked you why, and you said it was
nothing.

But plants were dying, and it was getting *so cold*,
and all you could do was tell me *not to worry*.
The truth is, the sun has gone out, my love,
and despite what you think,
this earth is on its last legs.
I've packed my bags.
The sun will never again rise,
and the plants will continue to wither,
if I stay,
so when you ask me why I'm leaving,
look to the empty sky.

MISTRESS MARY

I am known as **Mistress Mary**, and I am feeling
quite contrary as I stand here looking pretty, but feeling dirty.
Little Boy Blue will never blow his horn fast enough; my life is no
longer steeped in nursery rhymes. (*Look how the bath water glistens,
I find it very hard to listen to mother when my toys are there for me instead.
My life revolves around nursery rhymes.*)
Why don't you take a **Goosey Goosey Gander** at what
I've got under my dress? I'll ignore the frigid wind as it nips
at my body like the **Three Little Kittens** who've lost their mittens;
my life is no longer steeped in nursery rhymes. (*I love it when my
mother tucks me into bed, and when my daddy kisses my head. I can't wait to
hear tonight's story.
My life revolves around nursery rhymes.*)
Come on over **Georgie Porgie**, and let me show you
what a Mistress can do. If you're a real good boy, I'll let you ring my
Ding Dong Bell; my life is no longer steeped in nursery rhymes. (*My
dolls all have different names, and I love playing all types of different games,
mother says I have to come inside because it's going to rain.
My life revolves around nursery rhymes.*)
Polly Put the Kettle On I've had a pretty long day. **Roses are Red** and
I'm feeling dead, though I suppose tomorrow's another day. It's time

to **Rock-a-Bye Baby** so I might as well rest my head. As I close my eyes for a fleeting moment my life revolves around nursery rhymes. *(Dinner is served promptly at five, but everybody*
keeps yelling. I don't know how it got this way, there really is no telling.
Daddy slams his hand down, mother slams a door; my life is no longer
steeped in nursery rhymes.)

WOLVES AND THE MOON

Solemnity is called for, when the wolves
have suddenly stopped their howling
because they are (in love with the moon.)
She bathes the forest in her cool, pale light
watching the world with abandon
that speaks of (deep and true affection.)
Susurrus echoes of the wind through the
naked trees are undulating
through the ears of wolves (whose cries have stopped.)
Snouts raised to the stars that are covered by
heavy snow filled clouds, they wait for
the moon to come out and (bless their souls.)

3 AM

I can't breathe.
I don't know how to hold my head up,
how not to swallow this acrid sludge that
keeps forcing its way down my throat.
I can't hear.
If I listen hard enough, the silence is astonishing,
and it terrifies me, because I'm screaming,
I'm crying out for help and nobody can hear me.
But I can see.
I've never been blind, and I think that's what scares
me the most, the fact that I can see it all coming for
me until I can't breathe, and I can't hear; I am rendered
Helpless.

JACK WOLFE FROST

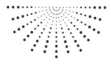

BIOGRAPHY

Jack Wolfe Frost is the Eternal Rebel; he rebels against everything which may have the word "rules" or "behave" within it. Born in Sheffield, UK, in 1956; he first started writing in 1982, as a hobby - Now older and wiser, he still seeks to break rules - and has had numerous poems and short stories published.   Jack Now lives In Clarksville, Tennessee. You can find Jack's meanderings on his blog at https://jackjfrost.wordpress.com/ and twitter at https://twitter.com/JackWolfeWriter

BITCH WITCH

Augusta's lips flashed a wicked smile,
As the asked if I would stay a while,
Her cauldron breath so hot and fierce,
And eyes that glowed and souls did pierce,
I said "Pray no, I must be home,
And fear I must but leave you alone."

Her face contorted in anger twisted,
And hissed a spell that me inflicted,
"You'll never leave until I say,
I've treats in store for you this day,
You'll do my bidding and be my slave,
Or your bones will rot in my deep cave."

My breathing rose and mind felt fear,
I've come so far and now I'm near,
I doubt now that my plan will work,
My hands can't reach a hidden dirk,
I wish I had instead but listened,
To those who doubted on my mission.

And so my bones rot in this cave,
Fester in this deep dark grave,
If you intend to kill this witch,
Remember –
She's an awful bitch.

AARON CHANNEL

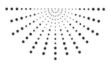

BIOGRAPHY

Aaron Channel is computer wiz and devoted family man. One of his biggest passions is being a chef and he is currently working on creating his own cookbook. He was recently accepted into the "Curses and Cauldrons" anthology by Blood Song Books.

THE LARK'S MELODY

Through doors locked
And windows barred
My soul walked
Past the stars
And I dance
To wordless tune
A second chance
For love of the moon
Light over the sea
Waves lapping gently
My heart dies
A silent scream
And I rise
From my perfect dream
To hardened reality
Somehow it seems
That I am still me
And I know why
The caged bird sings
Lord, I cry
And a caged heart screams....

PRAYER

For the child I once was
For the love I dream of
For the dead, cold in their graves
And the many nameless slaves
Who would be free
And that the Lord may live in me

For the miser, alone with his wealth
For the cancer patients' failing health
For the strong and for the meek
That they might find what they seek
And that the blind may someday see
And that the Lord may live in me

For the child born without a home
For those loved and those alone
For the old and for the new
For the many and for the few
That fear what may come to be
And that the Lord may live in me

For length of time
And strength of rhyme
For the alpha and the omega
For the lock and the key
And that the Lord may live in me
Just for today
For this I pray

LOVE

Like the strings of a lute,
Though silent at first,
Once plucked are never mute
They may fade at worst
At best, a crescendo of sound
Once lost, forever found
The strings, though they may ring with separate tune
Create a harmony like sun and moon
The music, at times, creates; at times, consumes
It may hurt, but never hate
Though discord may ring out
And our beautiful melody be lost amongst the shout
It still serves to bring silent harmony to our ears
And calm our horrid fears
Of separation and life diminished
With each new note is our love replenished

GHOST

I saw a young boy
I couldn't help but stare
And then
When I looked again
He wasn't there

I'm scared of him
Scared of what I see
But then again
I think he's scared of me

It's always eerie
Confronting a memory
I think he was me
Or, at least, who I used to be

I know
Because he had my eyes
Although
That's all I could recognize

He wasn't there again today
Sometimes I wish he'd go away

And then
I look again
I can't believe what I see
That can't be me?

He looks at me and cries
And I hardy notice the tears
In both our eyes
Will that really be me in a few years?

ASK ME

Ask me what it means to be free?
Is it a privilege to be taken away
Based on what we do today?

Ask me about liberty?
Ask if there's any price too great to pay
For the right to chose your way?
Ask what I would sacrifice
For a second chance at life?

And ask me about the endless ways
To count the bars of your cage
And the endless days
Upon endless days

Ask me how long
Can you stay strong
And what happens to your soul
When you lie forgotten in the hole

And, finally, you can ask me

How can I hold my head up high
When these bars and these prison walls
Will hold me
Until I die

I will answer
Shackles and chains can not
Can not a spirit break
And concrete and steel does not
Does not a prison make

A.R. JOHNSTON

BIOGRAPHY

AR Johnston is a small town girl from Nova Scotia, Canada. Her style of writing is considered Urban Fantasy.She participates in NaNoWriMo, won a Live Write and a contest for a "kiss scene" included in a novel of a best selling Indie author in 2018. Lover of coffee, horror flicks, and reader of books. She pretends to be a writer when real life doesn't get in the way. Pesky full time job and adulting!

IT BEGINS ANEW

And so it begins, the beginning of the end
I never thought it would come to this
But I won't ever bend
How had it all fallin' from bliss?

We had been the perfect semblance of love and grace
Years of affection and love
But now all you seem to do is debase
And now you've gone, given it all a shove

What the hell is this all about?
What did I ever do to deserve all that?
Did I ever go and act out?
We need to stop and not have another spat

I can no longer handle this animosity
I will no longer allow myself to feel this despair
I refuse to be part of this atrocity
In fact, I no longer care

I will not be left behind

I refuse to sit here and cry
I will no longer be so blind
I will no longer let my soul die

And so maybe this is not the end
It will be that I am going to soar
I will let my soul mend
It will be myself that I adore

I will love me forever more
No longer shall I be shy and cry
I will be the one that knows the score
So this is it, goodbye

ENCHANTED

It was all so new, bursting in my chest
My breath hitches
Tension starting to let go
Head going fuzzy and giddy

I couldn't help but feel alive
That fresh new feeling staying strong
The voice, the touch, sending tingles down my spine
Shivers making me grin

I couldn't wait to be touched again
The pleasure trailing across my skin
His fingers play across my body
Like a maestro creating music

Every strum and note is played
The touch making every nerve sizzle
The heat through my system like a slow burn
It was so very pleasurable

Over too quickly

Like a blink of the eye
I was soft and pliable
Being like clay that had just been sculpted

Reset and rested
Relaxed and calm
Like a puppet that had lost its strings
Time to slumber

JOHN GREY

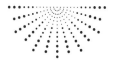

John Grey is an Australian poet, US resident. Recently published in Midwest Quarterly, Poetry East and North Dakota Quarterly with work upcoming in South Florida Poetry Journal, Hawaii Review and Roanoke Review.

FIENDISH

Finding your missing loved one
in the cellar of some fiend,
mouth gagged,
arms and legs bound to a chair,
is a rapturous feeling
beyond all known ecstasy
as you quickly undo her bindings
and she falls gratefully, adoringly,
into your arms.

But if she's been dead some years,
her flesh comes apart in your hands,
her grinning skull hangs
half-severed from her neck,
then the revulsion, the misery,
will be more than you can bear.

If you're the fiend however,
the reverse is true.

YOUR COMPANY IS REQUESTED

Don't leave
though you freeze my blood
at 2.00 A.M.
on an August night.

I praise the voice
that wails at me.
I adore the face
even as I see right through it.

Sure it's a performance by the dead
and reality would be better off without it

My memories have an investment
in these wispy ultimatums,
that dry-throat screech,
the wind-whipped moans.

Better an outraged phantom
than a rotting corpse,

a ghost of the half-light,
than a body in full glare.

THE CHILDREN EXPLORE THE OLD HOUSE

She found old wedding cake
in an icebox in the cellar.
It tasted like baked tar.
But she was hungry
so she ate it.

Her brother explored
the upper rooms.
The floor creaked
even when he stood perfectly still.

She spewed a few crumbs
all over the damp floor.
He thought he heard a noise
coming from the closet.

Must be a hundred years old,
she told herself.
I'm not afraid of ghosts
was his momentary
call to action.

She screwed up her face.
but she finished most of it.
He took a deep breath
and swung open that closet door.

The taste stayed with her for days.
She got off easy as it turns out.

SAM M. PHILLIPS

BIOGRAPHY

Sam M. Phillips is the co-founder of Zombie Pirate Publishing, producing short story anthologies and helping emerging writers. His own work has appeared in dozens of anthologies and Magazines such as Full Moon Slaughter 2, 13 Bites Volumes IV and V, Dastaan World Magazine, and Breach Magazine. He lives in the green valleys of northern New South Wales, Australia, and enjoys reading, walking, and playing drums in the death metal band Decryptus. A prolific poet, he writes to cope with existence and express feelings which may comfort others in times of strong emotion.

MUSE

Your pride wants to prescribe the words on this page,
The way that I express you,
But you cannot totally tyrannize me with lies,
And hide your true motives,
Emotive response comes alive in my eyes at your presence,
But this is no pretense,
I know who I contend with,
You would force me to bend,
And bow and cower,
And believe in the shower of inspiration as my own,
Ego grown and inflated,
Personality elated,
To fall under your gaze,
And be amazed at my own muse,

But it's you I use,
I bring you to life through me,
You will always be subservient,
Sure, I'm a convenient medium,
To escape from the tedium,

Of your ethereal existence,
But don't deceive yourself to believe,
That by persistence,
You lower my resistance,
And creep into my skull,
And push me aside,
Make me dull,

I'm a beacon burning bright,
A radiant soul in the night,
I bind you to my side,
And give you life for a time,
I'm your instrument,
A testament,
To who and what you are,
But you cannot bar me from my own voice,
It's my choice,
If you come through or not,
It is I who allow you to make my brain burn hot,

I'm not a vacillating lackey,
I'm a facilitating turnkey,
You're nothing without me,
So dictate these words,
They need to be heard,
I'll write them down,
And speak them in town,
I'll show your form,
Through words that adorn,
I'll let my body be worn,
But don't' believe you can scorn me,
I was born to be free,

So stand aside spirit,
I have my own merit,

Give me credit,
For being brazen and brave enough,
Strong and tough,
To handle your rough treatment,
To give testament,
For the sake of art,

But with this I start,
To realize,
Oh, muse,
It's me you use!
Abuse your power,
Cower behind false pretense,
A contest,
Between head and heart,
You start a war,
And keep score,
No law,
Nothing forbidden,
Only hidden context,

To vex me,
You hex me,
Confidently casting,
And blasting me with words,
Heard internally,
So that I don't suspect or become suspicious,
That the conspicuous calls come from you,
A parasite running parallel,
A hell in line with my own thoughts,
You contort and distort as a first resort,

To hide your true form,
The norm is for you to say you're me,
You'll always be inside my mind,

Filled with selfish guile and wicked wile,
You stay awhile and steal,
A massive mental meal,
As I lay passive and reveal,
My inner horde,
On which you gorge,
A forge of liquid steel,
On which you become drunk and reel,
Concealing self in baleful fire,
And wicked lies,
You are desire,
And more besides,

You are temptation and frustration,
Anger and rage,
You are the rattling, robust metal cage,
In which I'm trapped,
Clapped in irons,
Confined and refined,
Down to raw emotion,
It is the commotion itself that you feed on,
The cap you don,
And feel proud,
To have cowed,
A mighty soul such as I,
Left to cry and die by your words,

They are absurd,
But heard,
And identified with,
A course grained sieve,
Through which my entire life drains,
Sorts and retains,
The choicest tidbits,
The flailing fits,
On which you sip,

And slip and play,
Every day,
I'm forced to hear you and react,
Contract a virulent virus of the mind,
Muse,
You really are unkind.

BROWN GLASS PILL

Night,
Writhe on bed,
Pent up frustration,
No release,
Skin crawls,
Nerves frayed,
Nothing to placate,
All avenues spent.

Move to edge,
Feet on wooden floor,
Bend over double,
Noise bursts out of me like vomit.

Throat,
Rumble,
Grind,
Push,
Guts,
Tense.

This room is a cage,
This life, a cage,
Wanting out,
Suicide no option,
Can't go on,
Will go on,
No other choice
But to live with the pain.

Lash tongue,
Grind teeth,
Roll eyes,
Wring hands,
Kick feet,
All useless,
Write poetry,
Useless.

Brown glass pill,
Bitter,
Dense,
Fills me with rage,
Not enough,
Too much,
Is there anything that works?
Anything that doesn't turn on me?

Scream,
Rasp,
Bellow,
Snort,
Scratch,
Tear.

My flesh is wet paper,
My mind, concrete,

Electricity inside my veins,
Under the skin,
Behind my eyes,
Neck tense,
Back tense,
Muscles taut like cords.

I am alone,
For the best,
What use are you?

There's nothing to say,
What could possibly calm me?
A mood brought on from the outside,
I do not feel like I have any control.

I wish it would cease,
That is why I write,
For the feelings to be vented,
For them to be expelled,
Get out of me!
Flow onto the page.

Ink,
Blood,
Fury,
Light,
Burn,
Carve a path to freedom.

It boils in my chest,
Sears my throat raw,
Projects out like bile.

Raised hair and melt mouth,
Dry eyes and broken nails,

Who would come near this beast?

Alone,
Alone,
Alone,
Alone,
It is what I want,
Because you are no help at all,
You suffer too,
The two overlap,
I am no help to you.

We all suffer alone.

WAITING FOR THE STORM

Soon, a storm will come,
But it is not yet here.

Out one window is an idyllic scene,
Sunshine, green grass and forests,
Bright blue sky,
White, fluffy clouds,
High, thick and unmoving.

Out the other window,
A shadow hangs over the field,
Blue sky peeks through tiny gaps,
Fast moving grey clouds march low in the sky,
Drawing a curtain over the painting above.

I walk outside,
Over to the dirt road,
Ants, small, and smaller,
Hurry and fret,
Acute senses warn them,
Make preparations.

Towers of grass,
Islands of refuge among the sea of dirt,
A home for a lone lady beetle,
Red and black,
Unmoving, uncaring,
A ferocious battle tank in peace time.

A dragonfly,
Clear wings a blur,
Body a dash of brilliant green paint,
Hovers and darts,
Start, stop,
Among the grass,
Then away,
High into the sky.

A rumble overhead,
The sonorous call of thunder,
Echoing in the next valley,
Like distant cannon fire.

A tension in the air,
The heat sucked away,
Freshness on the nostrils,
A sudden stillness,
Only moments now.

Grey and black fills the sky,
Horizon to horizon,
The rumble more insistent.

Now, suddenly,
A fierce wind,
Rattles the windows,
The trees sway,

Kookaburras laugh,
Or warn each other.

I feel a point of moisture on my skin,
Then another,
Dark spots appear in the dirt.

Crack,
The sky opens,
Fury let loose,
Unloads water,
Life giver,
Life taker,
Elemental behemoth,
Washes away vision,
Covers me,
Covers all,
In a sheet of pelting rain.

PREY

Black bug,
Green spider,
Titanic battle,
Played out in miniature.

Flight, bite, sting,
Claws grasp,
Legs kick,
Roll across the table.

A blur of movement,
Two blended as one,
Locked in a death grip,
Who is the prey?

Green bulbous body,
Legs fall slack,
Dead.

Sharp black head,
Antennae flick,

Triumph.

Small bug drags larger spider to the edge,
Flight attempted,
Falls.

Both caught by an un-sensed web,
Legs kick frantically,
Panic.

A much larger spider moves in.

ROWANNE S. CARBERRY

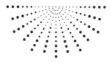

BIOGRAPHY

Rowanne S Carberry was born in England in 1990, where she stills lives now with her cat Wolverine. She has always loved writing, and her first poem was published at the age of 15, but her ambition has always been to help people which led her in a long journey. Whilst still writing Rowanne studied at the University of Sunderland where she completed combined honours of Psychology with Drama. She is hoping to soon gain her masters in counseling. She writes to offer others an escape and in doing so has published short stories, been accepted into various story anthologies and also into poetry anthologies. Although Rowanne writes in varied genres her favourite being fantasy, each story or poem she writes will often have a darkness to it, which helped coin her brand, Poisoned Quill Writing – Wicked words from a poisoned quill. Rowanne is currently working on several projects at the moment, both novels and poetry. When Rowanne isn't working or writing she reads the thousands of book that are still to be read, enjoys the gym, spending time with her family and friends, baking and binge-watching new TV series.

To keep in touch with Rowanne you can follow her on Facebook, Twitter, and Instagram.

GRIEF

Heart constricts with the vines of grief
Thorns dig in and tear at the pain
Thoughts of happiness stolen by a thief
From memories, you try to refrain

A tear falls like an acid drop
Burning where it lands
Nothing to do to make it stop
Except wipe it away with shaking hands

Screaming and raging at passers-by
Arguing over something so small
The reason for your rage you try to deny
Not saying goodbye will be your downfall

Calling their phone just to say hi
But there's no dial tone
And inside you die
As you remember the person has gone

It's all a nightmare; it's all a bad dream

You'll open your eyes and there they will be
But instead its shadows and you cry and you scream
As you know from this grief you will never be free

The guilt that you feel
That you let something make you smile
That you laughed and you joked and let out a squeal
And for a moment, you were happy, just for a while

Time goes on and memories fade
The sound of their voice has disappeared
Forgetting the lines of their face makes you afraid
Time goes on and everything changes as you feared

A missing piece from your heart
Leaves you never feeling whole
Knowing that forever you will always be apart
Each death of a loved one takes another part of your soul

WHAT COLOUR DO YOU BLEED?

If I slit my wrists,
And then yours too,
Would mine be black,
And yours be blue?

If I ripped open your chest,
And then ripped open mine,
Would yours beat ok,
But mine beat out of time?

If I pulled out my eyes,
And then did the same to you,
Would mine see lies,
Whilst yours see true?

If we both went to war,
But were on different sides,
Would we still be friends,
Or would we shoot one other as the dictators advise?

If we changed the way that we look,

And the colour of our skin,
Would it make it easier for others,
To see the person within?

If we took away the hatred,
That there is on the earth,
Would we still kill each other,
Or would we find that the other had more worth?

If I stripped away your skin,
And then stripped away mine,
Would I be made of darkness,
And you be made of sunshine?

If I slit my wrists,
And then yours too,
And our blood mixed together on the floor,
Could you tell me which belonged to you?

ADDICTION

You take another smoke,
And have another drink,
Everything around you turning into one big joke,
But another hit makes it so you don't have to think.

You hit your wife cause she told you to stop,
Begged and pleaded to not have them people in the house,
Your once happy daughter now quiet as a mouse,
But you don't care and go off in a strop.
Wake up in the morning in too much pain,
So you reach for drug to take it away,
Off your face again for another day,
Lost your job today and looking for someone to blame.
Try to visit your daughter but she doesn't want to see,
The man who hurt her mum,
And let her be touched by scum,
Whilst you sat in a chair to stoned to disagree.
No reason to wake and no reason to dress,
Sat on the couch with a can in your hand,
And a joint in your mouth,
Someone at the door "I want my money", they demand.

Everything gets worse,
But you don't feel you can ask for support,
So you sit in the dark and blame the universe,
Instead of holding out your hand, you take another snort.
Passed out again on the floor all alone,
Bottles all around and needle in your arm,
Need to call for help but can't reach the phone,
Found by your family, your call for help, your outstretched palm.

LIVING NIGHTMARE

Chased in the darkness by monstrous hands,
Forced to meet someone else's demands,
Whilst screaming inside for someone that understands.

Held down on a bed by shadows in the night,
Heart rate climbing from the growing fright,
Wishing her life was a story she could rewrite.

Cigarette burns littered across her in black,
Scores from a game of blackjack,
Are forever drawn into the skin of her back.

Horrors she thought that she would never see,
Humans and animals turned into something beastly,
Her death the only thing that would come with a guarantee.

Forced to be naked in front of groups of strangers,
Pushed into situations where there are thousands of dangers,
Wondering lost and alone in unknown chambers.

Eventually given a chance to be alone,

Kidding herself that she's grown a backbone,
But one look to the wall, shows an image of her gravestone.

An opportunity for dreams,
Only leads to more screams,
As she sees her blood flowing freely in streams.

She sits in a corner and she silently cries,
Knowing that everything she had been told was lies;
Nightmares don't only happen behind closed eyes.

JOANNE VAN LEERDAM

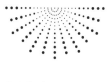

BIOGRAPHY

Joanne Van Leerdam is an Australian writer of horror, poetry, and occasionally fantasy stories. She lives near Warrnambool in regional Victoria, Australia, where she teaches senior high school English, History and Drama/Production. She is an active member and performer in Camperdown Theatre Company.

Her hobbies include reading, music, travel and photography.

Joanne loves travelling, and has visited many places in Australia as well as holidaying in New Zealand, Fiji, the USA and Canada at different times. Other than Australia, eastern Canada is her favourite place in the world, and she's proud to have been adopted as an 'honorary Canadian.'

Joanne is the author of thought-provoking and profound poetry, horror and short stories. She has won a number of awards for her books 'New Horizons', 'Nova' and 'The Silver Feather.'

FINALLY

For so long now
She has been waiting
For her mysterious prince,
Longing for him to carry her away.
He is ever present in her thoughts:
Oh, how she desires his embrace!
And yearns for his kiss that will change her forever
As she surrenders to him, heart and soul,
Finding in his arms her refuge from the world,
Preparing to fulfil her destiny
When she finally enters his kingdom,
Never to be separated from him again.
In her impatience
She has begged him
To hasten his preparations—
She cares little for palaces,
Or grand plans, or kingdoms.
All that has held her back
And held her down,
She will gladly leave behind
For those who prefer worldly goods

Over happiness and freedom.

Time drags its heels
As though deliberately seeking to thwart her hopes;
Hours and days blur into weeks
Marked by sighs and tears
As regular and constant
As the pendulum of the clock
Or its doleful horary chime.

Then, on a day that has until now been like every other,
Her vigil is rewarded.
The air in her lungs tightens
As her heartbeat echoes the pounding of hooves—
She hears them first, before he comes into view.
Although late in the day,
Sunlight shimmers yet on the fine fabric
Of his clothing and his royal standard,
Turning crimson to fire and black to brightness,
Igniting sparks on silver rings and buckles and stirrup,
That leap and streak like ribbons of lightning
Along the sleek sheen of his black stallion,
That proud and mighty destrier
That bears him toward her post haste,
Cloak billowing behind him as he rides.

The afternoon shadows have grown longer
Before the bustle of final preparations falls still.
She is ready, dressed for the journey:
Entertaining no desire to tarry there,
She makes fair haste, with a spring in her step
In time with the song of welcome
That she hums, though her heart would sing.

The door swings open as he alights —
Although some would bar his way, they dare not,

So at the threshold he stands before her,
Arms outstretched, beckoning to her,
Tenderly speaking her name.

With the radiance of the sun now captured in her smile
And reflected in her welling tears of joy,
She steps through the door of her father's house,
And reaches eagerly for those hands
Whose touch she has hoped for and dreamed of
Ever since that day, months ago,
When she first heard his name,
When she promised her future to him.
"My prince, you are here at last," she beams,
Her face radiant as his eyes hold her gaze
And he pulls her close to him.

He bends to meet her lips with his,
A kiss filled with love, hope and longing,
Therein speaking volumes that only they need know.
His fingertips caress her face,
Erasing the faint lines traced there by time and waiting.
"Come with me, my sweeting,
Make your home and your life in mine."

Her father and brothers step forward,
Faces filled with fear and distrust—
Blind to his beauty and wisdom,
They see only the darkness of clothing
That cloaks the man within.

Standing steadfast beside her prince,
She turns to those who would keep her there,
And, seeking to reassure them,
Smiles with gentle compassion for their misery.

"Do not fear for me, my brothers!

Beloved father, let me be free!
Do not condemn him without knowledge,
Or judge only on what you perceive.
I have lived here all my life, 'tis true,
Yet I have never been so fully alive
As I am now that my prince has come."

Turning to him, she gently touches his face
As a question spills from her lips:
"Why do they fear you, my darling,
When I have pleaded with you to come?
Why would they keep me from you
When I have longed so to be your own?"

"My sweet," he replied, "be neither angry
Nor saddened by their lack of grace:
People often suspect the darkness,
And things they do not know;
They seek to protect the ones they love,
And keep them safe and close."

"My love," she answered, "They need only know
The depth and sincerity of my regard,
The comfort and warmth that I find in your arms,
The joy with which I take my leave—
To accept your intentions are true."

She squeezes the hand in which her future is held,
As a signal she is ready to leave,
So he leads her through her final steps
Before lifting her tenderly onto his steed.

"Farewell, beloved father; do not weep, I pray,
And brothers - think kindly of me,
For I carry your love with me as I go,
And mine remains here with you forever.

Oh, I beg of you, do not grieve.

With movements graceful and well-rehearsed,
Her prince takes his place behind her,
And as he wraps his arm and dark cloak warmly
Around her small and delicate frame;
She smiles and waves her last goodbye
As he gently bears her away.

Thus she leaves the only home she has known,
Yet without sorrow or regret for those who remain.
For she fears neither the journey through the night
Nor her destination in that distant land
Of glorious eternal day.

IN A MEADOW BOUNDED BY ANCIENT TREES

In a meadow bounded by ancient trees
There stood, face to face, avowed enemies:
She, her royal father's heir, yet cruelly oppressed,
Her birthright held hostage at her rival's behest;
He, the minion of another, darker power,
Eager to glory in his quarry's final hour.

Beleaguered, exhausted, yet resolute,
Adana beheld the foul, monstrous brute—
Maddened by hatred, his fiendish eyes
Glazed over with bloodlust for his prize:
Her soul to appease his evil master's hate,
Her youthful flesh his own hunger to sate.

Behind him, myriad warriors thronged,
Armed by that fiend to whom they belonged.
Defiant, she glared at the seething horde,
Raised her chin boldly and lifted her sword;
"Begone, villains!" she cried, "Avaunt with ye!
Take thy judgement and conspiracy
Back to the darkness from whence you came,

That deadly kingdom of infamous name;
Tell thy vile Master I stand here, alone
Where he his visage has not shown,
And so, by default, this battle is won—
His devilish schemes are finally undone.
I field no soldiers, I command no knight
To preserve my honour or help me fight
Whatever army he has chosen to send;
By my own strength and merit, I will defend
My crown, my honour, my liberty—
Go hence, therefore, away with thee!"

His face contorted with malevolence,
And thus he spoke, in the tyrant's defence:
"Hold still thy strident tongue, and do not strive—
For only one of us shall leave here alive.
The hour of reckoning doth quickly approach,
And my dark lord cares nought for your haughty reproach."

"As thou dost wish," she replied, "but save your own breath,
For if, as thou sayest, this must end in death,
We shall fight, thee and I, until one must yield—
One on one, single-handed, in this very field;
For only a coward would wage war on a maid
With an army as surety for his crusade."

"Enough!" he growled, his eyes flashing with fire,
"Thou callest me coward, but thou art a liar!
A force gathers behind you, ready for war—
The rag-tag army of a troublesome whore.
Thou hast no more integrity than I—
Put off your pretence and prepare to die.

"They do not assemble on my command:
They seek justice and freedom for this ravaged land.
I do not lead or direct what they do,

Ask them thyself: they will tell thee it's true."

She neither looked back nor averted her eyes
But instead seized the chance to take him by surprise
When he glanced beyond her in a moment of doubt,
She overpowered him and turned him about,
Her knife at his gullet, to face his adherents
And held him with strength belied by her appearance,

"Arrogant fool! Hast thou never learned?
An angry woman should never be spurned.
Presume not that I cannot outfight a man:
Today thou shalt die as proof that I can.
Kneel before me, knave, and confess thy shame,
And bid your host of henchmen do the same."

"Never!" he cried, defiant and hateful,
Yet his eyes confessed his position was fateful
For he feared the wrath of his formidable foe,
Long fermented in hardship and seasoned by woe.

Stunned, his supporters made not a sound
As she forced her captive onto the ground,
Dagger still at his throat with deadly intent;
Livid with fury, her forbearance spent,
She flinched not as she drew her blade
Through flesh and bone, and thus she slayed
That agent of evil, the most noxious of men,
Who could never harass or pursue her again.
Her nemesis fell in a heap at her feet,
And, knowing her vindication was complete
She raised her bloodied knife up to the sky
And roared a victorious battle cry.
Shocked silence gave way to a groan of despair
From the soldiers of darkness still standing there,
Then, knowing their fortunes had swiftly reversed,

And with no-one to lead them, they slowly dispersed.

She stepped away from the corpse and its gore
Feeling lighter and freer than ever before,
Standing tall to address those who waited nearby
With her arms open wide and her head held high.

"As God is my witness, let it be known:
I hereby reclaim my kingdom and throne,
And vow to rule over this long-burdened land,
With justice and mercy in every command.
And you, loyal servants, shall be thus rewarded
For the trust your presence today hath afforded:
My knights, I appoint thee an honourable place
To counsel your queen with wisdom and grace;
My soldiers, I grant thee weapons and horses
And command of the kingdom's military forces.

While on the horizon, the sun sank down,
Adana knelt humbly to receive her crown;
Her new life as queen had this day begun:
The mistress of many and prisoner of none.

A.A. RUBIN

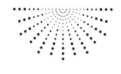

BIOGRAPHY

A. A. Rubin lurks in the shadows, for it is there that magic can still be found. You may have thought you saw him in the back of the bar, or going into the subway station, but when you looked back, he was gone. His work has appeared recently in journals including Kyanite Press, Pif Magazine, and Constellate Literary Journal. His story "The Substance in The Shadow" has been named a Fiction War finalist, and his story, "White Collar Blues" was nominated for the Carve Magazine/Mild Horse Press online short fiction award. Mr. Rubin holds a BA in Writing/Literature from Columbia University, and an MA in Teaching of English from Teachers College Columbia University. He can be reached on twitter and facebook @thesurrealari

FORTHWITH FLIES THE MAGE

There is a city on a hill
A beacon burning bright
A model of the great and good
A citadel of light

The enchanted forest lies below
Behind it mountains rise
Where darkness lurks inside the caves
And evil waits and hides

The city's ringed all around
By a wall both tall and stout
It glistens brightly 'neath the moon
And keeps the demons out

But Lo! The prince of devils stirs
He wakes, his power grows
He plots and plans his sweet revenge
The city does not know

He gathers spirits to his side

On that fateful day
And sends a sortie swiftly out
'Gainst the town to make assay

The wraiths are whirling all around
Above the city night
Attendant shadows do they bring
Quelling all the light

Forthwith flies the mage
On the dragon does he ride
Forthwith flies the mage
Through the dark and dusky sky

He brings his glowing staff to bear
And trains it on the shades
The dragon flaps its massive wings
Beating back the raid

The mage he speaks the sacred words
An ancient holy spell
The wraiths they writhe beneath his might
Banished back to hell

A raucous cheer, it rises up
From the city streets
Hosannas for the hero mage
Their enemies he beat

But deep inside the caves of hell
The demon king does rage
He stamps his foot and gnashes teeth
'Bout the failure of the wraiths

Sworn swords and lords he calls to him
He gathers up his hosts

A massive army to command
Of monsters, orcs and ghosts

They rise up like the living dead
And with a steady thrum
March to the heavy sound of doom
Beat out on their drums

The goodly people gather round
They cower in their homes
They pray to gods most tearfully
But fear they're all alone

Forthwith flies the mage
Resplendent in his power
Forthwith flies the mage
In the city's darkest hour

His dragon swoops with wings unfurled
It dives on down eftsoons
Towards the city's citadel
Silhouetted by the moon

Into the fray, callooh callay
Like Zeus' thunderbolt
He is the storm, Mjolnir thrown
Until he feels a jolt

His dragon's mighty scales are pierced
A bolt has found its mark
Shot blindly by a demon's bow
Lucky, in the dark

The dragon rears up suddenly
The mage from off him thrown
Falls straight down into the field

Through the Sturm und Drang

With magic does he slow his fall
And through the wind does float
And hovers lightly in the air
Above the city moat

Forward walks the mage
With a steady tread
Forward walks the mage
And faces the undead

He stands alone before the gate
His staff of yew in hand
The last best hope to stop the spread
Of shadow through the land

A silence settles o'er the field
The mage and the commander
Stare silently across the sward
Like figures trapped in amber

The demon lord's in disbelief
Have they just sent but one,
Hero 'gainst his mighty hoard?
They couldn't be that dumb

The devil lifts his first of doom
And gives the dread command
And thus the static silence breaks
At the falling of his hand

A volley from his archers flies
Into the sky of night
Eclipsing pale Hecate's orb
And quashing all the light

The arrows fall, a deadly rain
Toward the mage's person
The people groan behind the walls
His death is all but certain

The shafts they dot the city gate
Haphazardly they land
A raucous cheer now rises up
From the demon band

But still the single figure stands
When the air does clear
The mage, unscathed for all to see
Inside a glowing sphere

Another volley is sent forth
This one all-aflame
But when the arrows reach their mark
The outcome is the same

The demon prince, the lord of hosts
Rides up and down his ranks
His soldiers shout and beat their plate
Armor loudly clanks

And all at once the horde does charge
The wizard to engage
A cavalry of nightmares filled
With berserker rage

Forthwith flies the mage
Forward cross the field
Forthwith flies the mage
With just his staff to wield

He cuts on through the charging line
Breaking their formation
But round they move from the flanks
In retaliation

In the deadly circle stands
The mage with staff of yew
Surrounded by his evil foes
Whose vigor is renewed

Wave after wave they fall on him
In a constant motion
But break like water on the rocks
Which jut into the ocean

A ring around the mage does form
A pile of the dead
A mound of lifeless bodies grows
Even to his head.

They battle on past midnight
And still the bodies rise
A mountain there before the mage
Reaching toward the skies

The enemy indefatigable
Can smell the mage's blood
As he begins to tire
Drowning in the flood

The demon prince strides out perforce
To land the final blow
He gloats above the fallen mage
But little does he know

The injured dragon has returned

Seeking out his master
He swoops upon the hellish hosts
Reigning down disaster

Beneath their heavy plates of steel
The cavalry does burn
And with the fire of his breath
The tide again is turned

The mage's vigor is renewed
By his beast's return
Like the phoenix from the fire
His courage is reborn

He plants his staff and rises up
Trying to hide a wince
And looks into the demon's eye
Staring down the prince

The devil wields his ancient sword
Forged in the pits of hell
He swings it wildly at the mage
With an evil yell

The mage dodges dips and weaves
Avoiding every blow
But his leg is injured
And he drags behind his toe

The demon's rage redoubles
He sees the mage is lame
He focuses his efforts
On the leg that's maimed

But still the mage eludes him
Though each stroke by less

He wills his foot to movement
And curses 'neath his breath

The two contend throughout the night
The duel goes on for hours
They dig deep trenches in the dirt
Trampling all the flowers

The devils nicks him with his sword
The mage's hand drips blood
Which falls on down, to the ground
It's soaked up by the mud

The demon spins his spectral sword
His is the day to win
But his blade is frozen in the air
The mage breaks into a grin

He's drawn some symbols in the dust
With the leg that lagged behind
Tracing symbols runes in the dirt
Which the demon bind

And with the sacrifice of blood
Dripping from his hand
He locks the devil to the ground
Roots him to the land

The demon's hellish blood runs cold
He is a block of ice
The mage taps the ground with his staff
And mutters something thrice

The ground below does open
It swallows the prince whole
He sinks ever downward toward

The ancient pits of She'ol

The remnants of the demon horde
In confusion flee
The city gates are thrown open
With hurrah's and shouts of glee

But the field is empty
The mage he isn't there
He's mounted on his dragon and
He's flying through the air

Whenever he is needed
Wherever evil reigns
Take a look up to the sky
Forthwith will fly the mage

WHISPERS IN THE NIGHT

What's that voice outside my window
Is it a ghost or just the wind
Is just the leaves a rustling
Or are they whispering 'bought my sin
Rising up and spinning
In a column thin
Battling with my conscience
For my soul to win

ART AND CRAFT

When we're young
When we start
All that matters
To us is the art
But as we grow
And when we age
The craft then becomes
All the rage
This, it seems
Is the way
For Faulkner, Joyce
And Hemingway
And you, my dear
Must strive to bring
The golden mean
Between these things

NIGHT WALKERS

His life has been restored
But he hasn't been the same
His slurred and sloppy speech
Is calling out for brains
He grimly chugs along
Through the driving rain

I raise my zombie gun
And through the sight take aim
So he can rest is peace
And we can do the same

CHICKEN SOUP FOR THE LONELY SOUL

You may feel alone
But don't be distraught
Bet ya can't find me
Somebody who's not

So get out of your bed
Or get up from your seat
Get out of your house
And someone you'll meet

They may not be perfect
But you'll find in the end
You don't need perfect
You just need a friend

A LONE GIRL WALKS

A lone girl walks
Down a city street
People all around her
Whom she'll never meet
Her path is lighted
By an empty glow
From electric lights
For Broadway shows
She moves towards you
You catch her eye
But you're distracted
By something is the sky
A flashing add
On a giant screen
Promising
To fulfill your dreams
You wonder where
She had to go
But what's in her heart
You'll never know.

ANTHONY REGOLINO

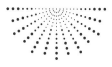

BIOGRAPHY

With over twenty years' experience in the publishing industry, mostly as an editor, Anthony Regolino has acted as ghostwriter and contributing writer, as well as creating professional blogs for company websites. His novel, *Canis Sapiens: The Dingo Factor,* was released in 2016, while his short story "The Mystified Morpheus" was included in the 2018 horror anthology *Fierce Tales: Shadow Realms.* While studying on scholarship in NYU's Dramatic Writing Program, he enjoyed seeing his first sketch performed before an audience—on Broadway, as he likes to say (which is technically correct)! Participation in local theater, both on and off stage, allowed him the opportunity to create an adaptation that was cleverly translated for the stage. He is currently working on having more of his works brought before an audience, in the form of prose, screenplays, teleplays, and comic book scripts. "The Duty" is his first published poem.

Visit him at https://www.facebook.com/anthony.regolino and at https://anthonyregolino.weebly.com.

THE DUTY

Heavily did the water weigh, upon her fragile form,
It crushed her down till none could see her if they stood above,
She understood full well this was the reason she was born,
A calling more important than the right to fall in love.

The fishes came to visit her, she knew them each by name,
But touch them she could not, for her hands could not leave the sword,
She could not move to swim with them or join them in their game,
She could do naught till she fulfilled her service to the Lord.

She knew the face belonging to the man who'd set her free,
It came to her when her eyes closed, so young, so proud, so fierce,
He knew not what she kept for him, nor what his fate would be,
Nor how he'd free her from the blade that her flesh it did pierce.

She'd smile when she'd recall the day that she had won the honor,
The sword went through her easily, it pinned her to the dirt,
The spell was cast, its magic true, the lake filled in upon her,
She did not bleed or breathe or eat; she felt not hunger nor hurt.

The land about her grew and aged, but neither could she do,
A maiden fair of fourteen years would be her lifelong state,
Preserved in holy water that was always warm and blue,
Awaiting he who's promised to be fair and just and great.

She'd give him what he needed to protect his kingdom best,
Relinquishing the power that abided in the lake,
She wouldn't know if he would be successful in his quest,
For not only the sword but her own life would he then take.

And when he finally came and looked into the clear still water,
There was no fear, no hesitancy, no regret in her heart,
He didn't know what she would hold; he just knew that he sought her,
To satisfy some prophesy, of which she was a part.

Her hands were finally free to move, ensuring she'd be found,
And when he grasped the weapon's hilt, he saw its metal gleam,
It drained the magic from the lake, the mistress, and the ground,
Causing the pool to roil and surge, and then begin to steam.

He pulled it from her body and then saw how it had staked her,
He backed away, absorbed with shock, retreating to dry land,
She smiled at him, then slowly vanished, off to meet her Maker,
Leaving him to marvel at the rust-free blade left in his hand.

"'Tis Caliburn," said Merlin, who had brought him to this site,
"The Sword of Kings, the Blade of Truth, the promise of our land,"
With it in hand Arthur was meant to enforce all that's right,
And be a shining beacon with a castle just as grand.

He looked back, wond'ring if the angel really had been there,
But naught was left to give credence to what he thought he saw,
A vision under water but with un-wet gown and hair,
Alive but yet not breathing, denying Nature's law.

She looked down on him, thrilled with her new angle of elevation,
Lacking a physical presence that a mortal could observe,
She gazed upon the waters that were formerly her station,
Then left the world of men to see how she could now best serve.

NERISHA KEMRAJ

BIOGRAPHY

Multi-genre (short-fiction) author, and poet, Nerisha Kemraj - resides in South Africa with her husband and two, mischievous daughters.

She has work published/accepted in 30 publications, thus far, both print and online.

She holds a BA in Communication Science from UNISA and is currently busy with a Post-Graduate Certificate in Education.

Visit her Facebook page for updates on her work.

WEB OF LIES

Beautiful threads of colourless hue,
laden with the morning dew
All interwoven,
without being broken

Linked together
So intricate
Web of lies
So delicate

She lies in wait
No need for bait
And soon they're trapped,
their energy sapped

As little as a tiny ant,
as mighty as a dragonfly
Once you're caught,
you can't deny
therein awaits
your last goodbye

I LOVE YOU

There's so many things I should have said,
But things got in the way,
Now, there's nothing I wouldn't give,
Just to hear you say:
I love you

You've gone across the ocean
to a land so far away
Miles and miles between us,
It's for your safety that I pray
I love you

For the love of your country
For the world to allay,
You risk it all,
in an act of brave display
I love you

It is you I wish to hold,
and not this sweet bouquet

Please return soon,
I prefer you to any lei
I love you

DOORMAT

I can feel the dirt sticking to me
Can you see it on my surface?
Do you see the way he walks all over me?
I don't think he does it on purpose...

All the laundry falls atop me,
and the food stains leave their mark
Is this what I was meant to be?
I feel like a useless benchmark

And now his friends all join him
Leaving footprints as they go
They ridicule me until the tears brim,
but no, I will not let it show

The world, all,
seems to laugh at me
But they don't know the strain
They don't see the wear-and-tear in me
Because to them I'm just a stupid doormat...
without a brain

Soon there'll be a replacement -
someone new to take my place
I secretly await displacement,
as I see the hate that plagues his face

But why do I still try?
Why am I holding on?
Why can't I say goodbye?
Maybe it's because they're right,
I've been just a doormat all along...

WHEN YOU

When you love someone so much,
waiting is a breeze
Whenever your souls touch,
wrongs are made right, with ease

Heaven's doors are opening
Hell's fires - all die down
He makes HER his queen,
he adorns a matching crown

Entwined, in each others love -
Even their hearts, both, beat as one
Engraving their love in the stars above,
ethereal magic has begun

Nearly every action spells bliss
No room for anger to stay long
Natural beauty from the first kiss -
nurturing their own love song

INNER BATTLES

Chemical shifts
Damaging drifts
Across the contours of my mind

Malignant guilt
Belligerence built
Bystanders are maligned

Internal fire
Murderous mire
Within myself – confined

THE END OF THEM

Like a moth drawn to a flame...
He knows he will be burned
but he can't seem to stay away

She, like the flame burning so bright
She knows she will destroy him
but he just won't take flight

Until they both burn out

NEW BEGINNING

It's time to step out of the dark
and prepare yourself to embark
on a journey that will spark
your inner spirit, a brand new path
Welcome change, forget the past,
things are never made to last
Let it go so you can start
a brand new life - out of the dark

MY WORLD

You're the centre of my universe,
The middle of my earth,
the core of my existence,
The soul of my birth

HAIKUS

Raindrops fill the void
an empty patio-chair
tell-tale handkerchief

Fragrant rose petals
Empty bottles, overflowing
blood-crimson on floor

J.E. FELDMAN

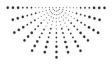

BIOGRAPHY

J.E. Feldman is one ancient soul reincarnate mixed with an enormous amount of inspiration, passion, and commitment. Her writing journey began at the age of three and has continued full blast with no sign of slowing down. She strives to continue writing and publishing six to eight books a year.

When not penning the next novel, she focuses on helping mentor authors, has a *Fantasy Writers* group on Facebook, and owns the traditional publishing company *Dragon Soul Press*.

The literature world is merely one of many facets to her life. She is fiercely passionate about vehicles and will one day be taking over the family's auto body business. In the meantime, she manages the shop and haunts car shows.

In her free time, J.E. enjoys road trips ripe with history, crocheting blankets for the homeless, and reading in cramped bookstores.

THE SWORD

Within meadows of green
A simple sword it may seem
Rising from stone in a field of dreams

Displaced from another life
It is as of yet unknown why
But it remains withstanding time

Day after day a maiden fair
Admired the sword while enjoying fresh air
Sensing bad weather she would bring a mare

Having hair golden as the sun
The dark townsfolk taunted and made fun
Until it was finally declared she was done

To the green meadows she did flee
For the solace she had under her favorite tree
There the parents found her with eyes full of greed

She was an orphan in strife

Unclaimed to be anyone's wife
And unfit to be given any kind of rights

She ran without knowing where
But they cornered her with a scare
"Stay away" was all she could declare

Stepped forward a woman and her son
"Halt, alone she may be but this girl is the one.
Legend has it she has only begun."

"Prove it is meant to be"
The townsfolk taunted with glee
The woman and her son knew then they would not see

To the maiden the woman said, "Save your life
By removing this sword and finishing the rite."
The stone suddenly seemed at a great height

The maiden, though confused, tied back her hair
With a schwick, the sword slid free and townsfolk stared unaware
That they who release it from the stone is named heir.

TITANIC

Music floats through the air across the water
As well as people - clinging to debris
No one hears their panicking cries
No one else sees the boilers falling apart
Or hears the glass of the once spectacular ship break

No one else saw almost all of the other
Passengers killed one by one
No one else awaited their fate that day
Only the passengers aboard that ship knew
What had truly happened

How come they perished and no one cares
Why were they left all alone, cold, and scared
How did they deserve this
At the bottom of the ocean they still await
But there was no savior for them

And there shan't be

FANNI SÜTŐ

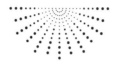

BIOGRAPHY

Fanni Sütő writer, poet, translator and the proud owner of a growing number of novels-in-progress. She publishes in English and Hungarian and finds inspiration in reading, paintings and music. She writes about everything which comes in her way or goes bump in the night. She tries to find the magical in the everyday and likes to spy on the secret life of cities and their inhabitants. Previous publications include *The Casket of Fictional Delights, Tincture Journal, Enchanted Conversation, Paris Lit Up 5* and *6*.

To learn more, visit www.inkmapsandmacarons.com

HEARTS MIGHT CHANGE

Hearts might change my dearest, didn't you know?
Follow the bunny; take me as your queen
I'll take you where the sweetest fountains flow
And show you the flowers man has never seen.
Hearts might change my dearest, didn't you know?

Hearts might change my dear, they become diamonds.
The prettiest ones lay deep in the mine.
Your will must be strong, harder than iron.
Then we'll eat candies and have some wine.
Hearts might change my dear, they become diamonds.

Hearts might change my dear, they change into clubs,
That we'll visit and bite the well-known apple
We sugarcoat it and consume our love
Then we sip manna and the juice of maple.
Hearts might change my dear, they change into clubs.

Hearts change my dearest, they change into spades,
they make deeper wounds than clubs when they thrust.

Flowers die when the army invades,
they attack to quench their raging blood … lust.
Hearts change my dearest, they change into spades.

GRANDMOTHER TIME

The world wasn't born in fire
It wasn't born in smoke
The big bang was just a legend
A bedtime story falsely told.
On a branch of the nothing – tree
Sits an old and ragged form
She knits and knits and knits all day
Never stopping, never bored
She is our old Grandma time
Knitting lives and stars and storms
She knits dragons she knits brave knights
And the whole of royal courts
Kings and queens and fools and all
You are yarn and I am yarn
One they we will all fall to threads
Being old and way too worn
But out of our shredded skins
New knitted stories will be born.